CANT

A GENTLEMAN'S GUIDE
TO THE LANGUAGE OF ROGUES
IN GEORGIAN LONDON

Stephen Hart

Improbable Fictions

Sydney, Australia

Improbable Fictions
contact@improbablefictions.com
www.improbablefictions.com

Book Layout ©2013 BookDesignTemplates.com

Ordering Information:
Quantity sales. Special discounts are available on quantity purchases by corporations, associations, and others. For details, contact the "Special Sales Department" at the address above.

Cant – A Gentleman's Guide to the Language of Rogues in Georgian London/ Stephen Hart. -- 1st ed.
ISBN 978-0-9924922-0-5

ACKNOWLEDGEMENTS

I would like to thank everyone who helped in the preparation and writing of this volume.

In particular I wish to thank my wife Pamela Freeman for her unfailing support and knowledgeable advice.

My thanks also to Andrew Taubman and Stephen Bourke for their many suggestions, all of which have improved this work immeasurably.

And finally, I would like to thank the late Mr Jonathan Wild, master criminal of the early 18th century, who first inspired me to study Thieves' Cant and without whom this book would undoubtedly never have been written.

TABLE OF CONTENTS

CHAPTER ONE

Introduction

Planning to visit Georgian London? You've collected some period money, got yourself kitted out with the appropriate clothes and had your inoculations. You have had your inoculations, haven't you? If not, go and do it right now. There are some nasty diseases and the environment is not healthy.

But one thing is missing. As well as the grand buildings in the West End, you want to see something of the seamier side of life. To do this, you have to blend in, and to blend in you have to know the language.

Canting, Flash Lingo, St Giles' Greek, Pedlars' French - the language of the London Underworld. You need more than just a few words.

Frankly, you can go into a flash ken and say bene darkmans but unless you can tell a clapperdogeon from a running smobbler the dambers will know you're half flash and half foolish and if you don't buy a brush the upright man will turn you over to a miller and you'll be taking an earth bath in a wooden surcoat before you know it.

Fortunately, you can avoid this fate with a little effort. A few hours study of this volume will enable you to pass as a bowman prig, even in the lowest company.

Don't be a sapskull. Carry it with you at all times.

Digressions

At intervals in this volume I have digressed into other topics that I think you may need to know to make your trip a more enjoyable (and survivable) experience. If you have done your own research before setting out, feel free to skip them. I shall not be insulted.

Stalling the Rogue

There is a very ancient ceremony called *Stalling the Rogue* to initiate a candidate into the society of rogues. It is described as follows:

The upright man takes a gage of bowse and pours it on the head of the rogue to be admitted; saying:

I, A.B. do stall thee B.C. to the rogue; and from henceforth it shall be lawful for thee to cant for thy living in all places.

It is unlikely that you will ever be *stalled* but at least when you have read this book you will know who the upright man is, the nature of bowse and why you might want a gage of it. And you never know. Strange things can happen in big cities and Georgian London is one of the biggest and strangest on the planet.

CHAPTER TWO

Getting Started

Greetings

Bene Lightmans	Good day
Bene Darkmans	Good night
How dost do my Buff?	How are things going?

Lightmans and *Darkmans* are, of course, the Day and the Night. Night may also be referred to as *Blindman's Holiday*.

Bene means good. *Buff* here is an adjective with man (or cove etc) implied. A buff person is one who stands buff - is strong and reliable.

Depending on the time of year, you can comment that the weather is *Ard* (hot) or *Znees* (frosty) or that there is a *Scotch Mist* (soaking rain).

Even among rogues, a comment on the English weather is always an acceptable way to start a conversation.

Good and Bad

Bene or *Bien* (pronounced 'bean') is a general term for good. Comparative (better) is *Benar* and Superlative (best or very good) is *Beneship*. It can be used in many contexts:

Bene Bowse	Good beer or strong liquor
Bene Cove	A good companion
To Cut Bene Whids	To speak gently
To Pike on the Bene	To run away while you can (in modern parlance, get out while the going is good)

A similar term is *Rum*. The modern meaning has shifted to mean 'Odd' but in Georgian England it means 'Good'.

Bene generally applies to people; *Rum* applies to things, although the rule is not absolute. For example:

Rum Prancer	A fine or beautiful horse
Rum Kicks	Breeches with gold or silver brocade
Rum Clout	A fine silk handkerchief
Rum Nab	A good hat
Rum Nantz	Good French brandy

The opposite term is *Queer* meaning bad.

Queer can apply to both people and things.

Queer Prancer	An old, worn out horse
Queer Kicks	A pair of old and tattered breeches
Queer Clout	An old handkerchief
Captain Queernabs	A shabby-looking man in poor clothes
Queer Cull	A fop or a fool

A rogue may be referred to as a *Queer Cove*. In this sense it is descriptive rather than pejorative. It can be used to describe roguish activities. For example:

Queer Cole Maker	A maker of false coins
Queer Plungers	Rogues who pretend to nearly drown and then try to extract money from Humane Societies and others
Queer Rooster	An informer

Men and Women

The terms for men and women are extensive and will be covered in more detail in later chapters. The following are a few of the basic terms:

Cove or Cull	A man
Swell	A gentleman
Mort	A woman
Gentry Mort	A gentlewoman

Now that you have a general idea of how this works, it is time to dive in and start learning some serious vocabulary. Alcohol is always a good place to start.

CHAPTER THREE

Buying a Drink

Time travelling is thirsty work so, shortly after arriving, you are likely to need a drink. The terms alehouse (which sells drink only), tavern (food and drink) and inn (food, drink and accommodation) are perfectly acceptable but there are some other terms you may hear, which are presented below. Georgian London has hundreds of these establishments. You should have no trouble finding one.

There are a large number of terms for drink and drinking. Whilst there is no need for you to use them all, you should at least recognise the terms when you hear them. Don't forget that you can use *Bene*, *Rum* and *Queer* as additional descriptors. A *Bowsing Ken* is an alehouse but if you like it you can describe it as a *Bene Bowsing Ken*.

Digression: Taverns

There are one or two taverns that might be of special interest to the gentleman time traveller.

The *Mitre* in Fleet Street was Dr. Johnson's favourite supper-house and his coterie included Oliver Goldsmith, Thomas Percy, John Hawkesworth and James Boswell. If you are in the mood to be richly insulted by an eminent lexicographer you need do no more than attempt to interrupt the good Doctor's dinner.

The *Rose Tavern* in Covent Garden was a favourite venue in the early Georgian period for dramatists and poets. Poet and playwright John Gay (famous for *The Beggar's Opera*) was a patron.

One inspired if drunken evening, Gay and his friends concocted a popular love ditty, entitled *Molly Mogg of the Rose*, in compliment to the then barmaid.

The *Rummer* is located between Whitehall and Charing Cross. If you are in London before November 7th 1750 (when it burned down) it is well worth a visit.

It is, among other things, the site of the first recorded robbery by escapologist Jack Sheppard (executed in 1724) from whence he stole two silver spoons.

If you happen to be in Pall Mall on 26th January 1765 and aren't upset by the sight of blood, you might care to visit the *Star and Garter* and check out the duel/drunken brawl between Lord Byron (the 5th Baron and grand-uncle of the more famous poet) and his soon to be late friend Mr Chaworth.

In an undignified scuffle in one of the rooms, Byron ran his sword through his opponent's stomach, causing him to expire the next day.

More importantly, in 1774 the tavern was the meeting place of the first cricket club where Sir Horace Mann (Kent), The Duke of Dorset (Surrey) and Lord Tankerville (Hampshire) laid down the first set of rules of the game.

If you are interested in boxing, the *Castle Tavern* in Holborn is, in the later Georgian period, a must see. It was the headquarters of the Prize Ring, kept by two of its heroes, Tom Belcher (until 1828) and, thereafter, Tom Spring.

The Daffy Club was inaugurated here by a Mr James Soares for its members to enjoy gin (daffy) and sports. It met in the long room beneath the portraits of pugilistic heroes, including Jem Belcher, Burke, Jackson, Tom Belcher, Joe Ward, Dutch Sam, Gregson, Humphreys, Mendoza, Cribb, Molyneux, Gulley, Randall, Turner, Martin, Harmer, Spring, Neat, Hickman, Painter, Scroggins and Tom Owen and also Jem Belcher's dog, Trusty, who apparently rated in this august company.

If you want to try your luck in low company you can visit the *Queen's Head* in Duke's Court, Bow Street but more study of this guide is recommended before you do so.

If you don't know what you are doing you are likely to *Catch a Cold* or get into trouble.

Don't *Sit on Thorns* - we shall get there soon enough.

The tavern is known locally as the *Go Shop* due to their serving gin and water in three-halfpenny bowls known as *Goes*.

Inns and Taverns

Bowsing Ken	Alehouse (literally Drinking Place)
Touting Ken	Alehouse (refers to Innkeepers touting for custom)
Hedge Tavern	A small, obscure tavern; also one frequented by sharpers (dishonest gamblers)
Flash Ken; Flash Crib	A tavern frequented by rogues
Mumpers' Hall	A tavern frequented by beggars
Stop Hole Abbey	The nick name of the chief rendzvous of the canting crew

If you think the landlord will let you run a tab you can ask to *Hang it up* or to *Walk up the Wall*. At the end of the evening you pay your *Scran*.

If you really want to be popular you can offer to *Stand Huff* or pay for everyone's drinks. The alternative, to *Lush at Freeman's Quay*, is to drink at another's expense, but this is seldom as well appreciated.

Tavern Workers

Beggar Maker	Publican or alehouse keeper
Bluffer	Innkeeper
Flash Cove or Covess	Landlord or landlady of a flash ken
Draper; Ale Draper	Alehouse keeper
Dash; Rum Hopper	The man who draws beer or other drinks
Neck Stamper	A pot boy

Note that an innkeeper can be referred to as a *Buffer* rather than a *Bluffer*. However, as this is also a term for dog, it is best avoided.

Drinks

There are many different terms for drink.

Booze; Bowse; Bub; Fuddle; Guzzle	General term for drink
Taplash; Wibble	Poor quality drink
Christened; Baptised	Drinks that have been watered
Bene Bowse; Cup of the Creature; Suck; Swizzle; Tipple	Strong liquor
Balderdash	Adulterated wine

Beer, Brandy, Gin and Wine

Belch; Bub; Hum Cap; Knock Me Down; Nappy Ale; Oil of Barley; Sir John Barleycorn; Stingo	Strong beer
Act of Parliament; Rot Gut; Water Bewitched	Small (heavily watered) beer
Bingo; Blue Ruin; Blue Tape; Daffy; Diddle; Drain; Frog's Wine; Geneva; Heart's Ease; Jackey; Lady Dacre's Wine; Lightning; Max; Rag Water; Sky Blue; South Sea Mountain; Strip Me Naked; White Ribbon; White Tape; White Wool	Gin
Cold Tea; Cool Nantz; French Cream; Red Ribbon; Rum Nantz; Red Tape; Suit and Cloak	Brandy
Black Strap; Kill Priest; Red Fustian	Port or sometimes claret
Bristol Milk	Sherry
Rum Gutlers	Canary wine

The most popular drinks are beer or ale, gin and brandy, but many drink wine and there is a variety of punches.

Beer needs to be divided into strong beer and small beer - the latter being quite dilute. The enormous popularity of gin is shown by the number of different terms for it.

Don't worry if you can't remember all these terms. A general selection will suffice.

Digression: Gin

The 'Glorious Revolution' of 1688 brought William of Orange to the British throne. Accompanying him on the ship was an uninvited guest but her presence was so familiar that no one commented on it. Her name was Madame Geneva, more commonly known in the short form - Gin. Distilled alcohol flavoured with juniper berries, it was encouraged by successive governments, which at the same time were restricting the imports of French brandy.

As the 18th century got going, gin became more and more popular and drunkenness became common to the point of affecting the economy through lost labour. Moralists and politicians joined forces to try and bring this foreign lady to heel but she refused to go quietly.

Compared to malt distilling (for, say, whiskey), producing gin is fairly simple and it could be produced cheaply in back rooms. When an Act in 1729 attempted to tax gin, the excise men had the devil's own job tracking where it was being made. Moreover, the Act defined gin as spirits to which juniper berries had been added. The rogues of London, no fools, simply left out the juniper berries and carried on. The poorer people of London were prepared to drink what was effectively raw spirit if it were cheap enough.

Determined to dig itself into a hole, the Government, in 1736, brought in punitive taxes of 20 shillings to the gallon and required £50 for an annual licence to sell gin. People ignored it.

Informers were encouraged at £5 a time. This resulted in the Magistrates' Courts being nearly overwhelmed, organised gangs of informers, mob riots and lynchings (of said informers).

The government introduced more and more harsh measures to even less effect. The Riot Act was read and the mobs ignored it. Madame Geneva's supporters were manning the barricades.

In 1751, Josiah Tucker of Bristol calculated that the annual amount gin cost the economy was three million, nine hundred and ninety-seven thousand, six hundred and nineteen pounds, and eleven pence halfpenny. While it is a wonderful example of spurious accuracy, the round sum of four million pounds is still impressive.

Sanity eventually prevailed. The Gin Act of 1751 cut licences and excise down to almost nothing and suddenly it became easier to do things legally. There were restrictions on precisely who could get a licence and it took a while to come fully into effect but by the end of the 1750s the Lady had achieved respectability and had settled down to become a tolerated member of society.

Other Drinks

All Nations	The drainings of the last drops of all bottles collected in a single bowl
Bragget	Mead and ale sweetened with honey
Cobbler's Punch	Treacle, vinegar, gin and water
Grog	Rum and water
Huckle my Buff; Twist	Beer, eggs and brandy, served hot
Kill Devil	Rum
Punch	Spirits, water, lemon and sugar
Purl	Ale with a dash of wormwood
Purl Royal	Canary wine with a dash of wormwood
Toddy	Rum, water, sugar and nutmeg

Non-alcoholic Drinks

Cat Lap; Chatter Broth; Congo; Gruts; Prattle Broth; Scandle Broth; Slop	Tea
Twist	Half tea and half coffee
Mahometan Gruel	Coffee

Three pieces of advice:

- Stay away from cheap gin - it is generally adulterated and may kill you
- Don't drink *All Nations* unless you have a really strong stomach
- If you are drinking *Purl*, make sure the *Bluffer* goes easy on the wormwood

Vessels and Quantities

Gage	Pint or quart
Nip; Size of Ale	Half pint
Cogue; Shove in the Mouth	Dram
Bouncing Cheat	Bottle
Bawdy-House Bottle	Small bottle
Soldier's Bottle	Large bottle
Scotch pint	Quart Bottle
Flicker; Romer	Drinking glass
Bubber; Whiskin	Drinking bowl
Clank	Silver tankard
Rum Clank	Large silver tankard

Glasses or bowls that are full to overflowing are called *Bumpers* or *Facers*. Empty bottles may be referred to as *Dead Men* or *Marine Officers* (the latter being regarded as completely useless by other seamen).

Make sure you hang on to any tankard you are served with. If a *Clank Napper* (a thief who steals tankards) runs off with it you may be blamed and have to pay the cost of replacement.

Levels of Intoxication

Stages of drunkenness range from the early, cheerful stages (*Chirping Merry*) to total incapacity (*Floored*).

Bit by a Barn Mouse; Chirping Merry; Hickey; Mellow; In a Merry Pin; Tipsy	Lightly intoxicated
Drop in His Eye; Half Cut; Half Seas Over; Sucky	Getting drunker
Boosey; Been in the Sun; Bowsy; Corned; Got into the Crown Office; Cup-Shot; Cut; Disguised; Flawed; Flustered; Foxed; Hocus; In his Altitudes; In the Gun; Nazie; Pogy; Pot Valiant; Bought the Sack; Top Heavy	Drunk
Clear; Deep Cut; Cut in the Back Leg; Drunk as David's Sow; Drunk as a Wheelbarrow; Drunk as an Emperor; Floored; Maudlin Drunk; Surveyor of the Highways; Swallowed a Hare	Very drunk
Crop Sick; Womble-Ty-Cropt	Hung over

A drunken man may be described using any of the above. He may also be described as a *Bingo Boy* (or *Mort* if a woman), an *Ensign Bearer*, a *Guzzle Guts*, a *Piss Maker*, a *Swill Tub*, a *Tickle Pitcher*, a *Toper* or a *Toss Pot*.

An excess of liquor may result in any of the following:

Cast up your Accounts; Cat; Flash the Hash; Cascade; Shoot the Cat; Flay the Flea; Flay the Fox	Vomit

Watch out for anyone described as a *Vice-Admiral of the Narrow Seas* - it refers to a drunk who urinates under the table into his companions' shoes. Sit near somebody else. Also, don't be a *Rat* (get taken up by the Watch when drunk) - the overnight accommodation in the watch house is most uncomfortable. Better not to get more than *Half Cut* if you can manage it.

Remember that a *Gage* can be either a pint or a quart. If in doubt, stick to *Nips* (half-pints).

CHAPTER FOUR

Money

Before we go any further it is time to discuss money.

For anyone used to a decimal system, the old English Imperial units can be a little tricky. Your basic unit is the penny. There are twelve pennies to the shilling; twenty shillings to the pound or twenty-one shillings to the guinea. A quarter of a penny is known as a farthing. Four pence is called a groat. Five shillings is a crown and... oh never mind, you'll soon pick it up.

Balsam; Bit; Blunt; Bunce; Bustle; Chink; Cly; Cole; Crop; Derbies; Dimmock; Dust; Gelt; Ginger-Bread; Iron; Kelter; King's Pictures; Loure; Muck; Poney; Prey; Quids; Rag; Recruits; Rhino; Ribbin; Stephen	Money in general
Goree	Money, usually gold
Plate	Money, usually silver
Lurries	Money but also small valuable items (rings etc)

Coins and Amounts of Money

Fadge; Grig; Jack; Mopus; Rag; Scrope	Farthing
Baubee; Brads; Grocery; Mag; Make; Mopus	Halfpenny
Win; Winchester	Penny
Dace; Deux Wins; Deuce	Twopence
Threpps; Thrums; Tres Wins	Threepence
Croker; Flag; Half a Hog	Groat (fourpence)
Bender; Cripple; Crookback; Pig; Sice; Simon; Syebuck; Tanner; Tilbury; Ill Fortune	Sixpence
	Nine pence
Bob; Borde; Hog; Jogue; She Lion; Twelver	Shilling
Loon Slate	Thirteen pence halfpenny
George; Half an Ounce; Fore Coachwheel; Slate; Slot; Trooper	Half a crown
Bull; Bull's Eye; Coachwheel; Decus	Crown (5 shillings)
Spangle	Seven shillings
Half a Bean; Half a Quid; Smelts	Half a guinea (ten shillings and sixpence)
Heart's Ease; Strike	Twenty shillings
Bean; Canary Bird; Goldfinch; Yellow George; Job; Megg; Quid; Yellow Boy	Guinea

Unless you are in the latter end of the Georgian period, do not refer to sovereigns. The first one was not minted until 1817.

Banknotes

Depending on which part of the Georgian period you are visiting, you may not have much contact with banknotes.

The first fixed amount notes did not appear until 1725 and the smallest denomination was £20. The £5 note was not issued until 1793 and the £2 and £1 notes not until 1797.

As a consequence of this, there are very few cant terms for banknotes.

Flimsies and *Screens* are the main ones, with *Queer Screens* referring to forgeries.

Rag, normally the term for farthing, is also sometimes used for banknotes.

Pecuniary Status

Chicken Nabob	One returned from the East Indies with a moderate fortune of fifty or sixty thousand pounds
Dipped	In debt, pawned or mortgaged
Dished Up	Totally ruined
To make Ducks and Drakes of one's money	To throw it idly away

Goldfinch	One who has commonly a purse full of gold
Plump in the Pocket; Warm; At High Tide; At High Water; Well Inlaid	Rich, in good circumstances
At Low Tide; At Low Water	When there is no money in a man's pocket
Outrun the Constable	In debt through living beyond one's means

More whimsical terms are *Gentleman of Three Ins* - in debt, in gaol, and in danger of remaining there for life and *Gentleman of Three Outs* - without money, without wit, and without manners.

Monetary Transactions

Apothecary's Bill	A bill for a great many items
Blood for Blood; Chop	Barter
Come	Lend
A Draught on the Pump at Aldgate	A bad bill of exchange
Flemish Account	A losing or bad account
Long-Winded Paymaster	One who takes long credit
Round Dealing	Plain, honest dealing
Smithfield Bargain	A bargain whereby the purchaser is taken in
Take French Leave	Run away from your creditors

CANT – A GENTLEMAN'S GUIDE | 23

Borrowing Money

Hopefully, you have provided yourself with enough money but if you find you have *Outrun the Constable* and your affairs are at *Low Tide* and you cannot *Touch* a companion for funds, you may need to *Break your Shins* and visit a *Two to One Shop* or a *Ten in the Hundred*. Or, in simpler language, you need to visit a pawn broker.

Breaking Shins	Borrowing money
Dun	An importunate creditor
Touch	Borrow from an acquaintance
Lay on the Shelf; Lay up in Lavender; Spout; Shove up the Spout; Vamp	Pawn an item
Two to One Shop	Pawnbroker
Cent per Cent; Ten in the Hundred	Usurer
Gullgroper; Impost Taker	Usurer who attends gaming tables and lends money at exorbitant rates
Hark-Ye-ing	Whispering on one side to borrow money

Goods that are pawned for greater than their actual value are known as *Pursenets*. In return, the money must be repaid at an exorbitant rate of interest. The young men who take up these offers are known as *Rabbit Suckers*.

Disposing of Stolen Goods

Although you should not be doing this yourself, if you are keeping low company you will frequently find that your companions raise money via the disposal of stolen goods.

Fence; Lock	A buyer of stolen goods
Lock; Stalling Ken	Place for receiving stolen goods - a fence's house or shop
Lumber House	A house used by thieves to store stolen goods
Lumber	Deposit property at a pawnbroker's, or elsewhere, for security
Plant	The place where stolen goods are secreted, either in the fence's house or elsewhere

Note that in the early Georgian period, *Fence* can simply mean spend as well as dispose of stolen goods. Be sure of the context before you use or interpret it.

Spending Money

Melt	Spend
Penny Wise and Pound Foolish	Saving in small matters, extravagant in great

Forgery

There are two main methods of coin forgery in use in the Georgian period - minting and clipping. Minting involves casting false coins in base metal. Clipping refers to shaving metal (silver or gold) from a coin, selling the resulting metal (or forging it into new coins) and then buying goods with the original coin at its full face value.

Good money is referred to as *Rum*, bad money as *Queer*.

Browns and Whistlers	Forged farthings and halfpennies
Button	A forged shilling
Nips	The shears used for clipping
Queer Bit; Queer Cole; Shan; Swimmer	Base or forged money
Queer Screens	Forged banknotes
Curle; Nig; Parings; Queer Cole; Shavings; Tower	Clipped coins
Smash	To pass counterfeit money

A *Nigler* is one who clips coins; the process is called *Nigging*.

A *Figure Dancer* is one who alters figures on bank notes, converting tens to hundreds.

Under no circumstances get involved in the forgery of money. It is not just a felony, it is High Treason and remains so until 1832. If convicted you will be drawn on a sledge to the Tyburn gallows, hanged then cut down, have various body parts cut off and eventually have your body chopped into quarters. Generally speaking you will not be cut down from the gallows until you are dead, but you might be unlucky.

CHAPTER FIVE

Food

The majority of people in Georgian London, particularly earlier in the century, do not cook. They have no facilities for doing so.

There are plenty of eating establishments and take-away food abounds.

It is time to visit a *Hand and Pocket Shop*, an establishment that will provide food in return for ready money. You can find them everywhere.

Digression: the Dangers of Food

There is a profession you hardly ever see in Georgian London - food inspector. You should think through the implications of this before going out and ordering food.

With a burgeoning population, food suppliers can sell everything they can get their hands on.

Many are unable to resist the temptation to bulk it up a little, to give it nice colours, to give it taste and, as we are in the days before refrigeration, to disguise rotting meat and fish.

Here are a few examples:

- *mustard powder*: mixed with flour and turmeric
- *cheese*: coloured with red lead
- *coffee*: adulterated with burnt sugar, acorns and mangel-wurzel
- *tea*: coloured with copper or black lead
- *bread*: whitened and bulked up with alum, plaster of paris, pipeclay and ground-up bones
- *wine*: mixed with sugar or lead to improve its taste

Ancient sides of beef can have fat applied which is then polished to make it look fresh. Fish gills can be painted with red lead to give them a fresher look. Anything and everything can be a cheat.

As for pies, the only way to be safe is not to eat them. Really. Just don't. Consider, if you will, how the term *Bow-Wow Mutton* came into being.

As far as possible, try not to eat the cheapest food. You will still end up devouring harmful chemicals, exotic bacteria and intestinal tract parasites, but you should survive. Do remember to have a thorough medical checkup when you get back.

Hunger and Thirst

If you are hungry and thirsty you need to be able to say so. As with drunkeness there are degrees, from mildly *Peckish* to completely *Gutfoundered*, or from suffering a *Stomach Worm* to having a *Wolf in the Stomach*.

Banded; Peckish; Stomach Worm	Hungry
Clammed; Gutfoundered; Wolf in the Stomach	Very hungry
Chapped	Thirsty
Long Stomach	A voracious appetite

A great eater is described as a stout *Trencher Man* or a *Knight of the Trencher*. He may be said to *Yam* his food. *Lenten Fare*, on the other hand, describes a sparse meal. Eating in general is called *Yaffling*.

Ingredients

The following represents the type of ingredients you may find in your food.

Bloody Jemmy; Knapper's Poll	Sheep's head
Bow-Wow Mutton	Dog's flesh
Cackling Farts	Eggs
Cash; Cassan; Caz	Cheese
Grannam	Corn
Grunting Peck	Pork or bacon
Irish Apricots; Munster Plums; Murphies	Potatoes
Pannam	Bread
Ruff Peck	Bacon
Sand	Moist sugar
Spread	Butter
Trundlers	Peas
Yarum	Milk

Birds

Biddy; Cackler; Cackling Cheat; Galaney; Margery Prater	Chicken
Bubbly Jock; Cobble Colter; Gobbler	Turkey
Quacking Cheat	Duck
Roger; Tib of the Buttery	Goose
Swish Tail	Pheasant

Farm Animals

Battener	Ox
Blater; Essex Lion; Quaking Cheat	Calf
Dunnock; Mower	Cow
Scot	Young bull
Long One	Hare
Ground Squirrel; Grunter; Grunting Cheat; Swing Tail	Pig
Sounders	Herd of swine
Bleating Cheat; Havil; Wooly Bird	Sheep

Dishes

Any or all of the following you can find at a good eating establishment. It is common to serve parts of an animal that are only rarely served today, such as sheep's head and an assortment of organs and intestines.

Alderman	Roasted turkey garnished with sausages
Crowdy	Porridge
Devil	Gizzard of turkey or fowl, scored, peppered, salted and broiled
Field Lane Duck	Baked sheep's head
Galimaufrey	Dish made from leftovers and scraps
German Duck	Half a sheep's head, boiled with onions
Grunter's Gig	Smoked pig's face
Hasty Pudding	Oatmeal and milk boiled and eaten with sugar and butter
Hodmandods	Snails in their shells
Poplers	Pottage
Salmon Gundy	Apples, onions, veal or chicken, and pickled herrings, minced fine and eaten with oil and vinegar
Scratch Platter; Taylor's Ragout	Bread sopped in oil and vinegar into which cucumbers have been sliced
Sugar Sops	Toasted bread soaked in ale, sweetened with sugar and grated nutmeg; eaten with cheese
Watch, Chain and Seals	Sheep's head and pluck
Bum Charter	Bread soaked in water

Note that the term sandwich was not in use until 1762 when it was popularised by the Fourth Earl of Sandwich, John Montague. You can still get one before this date but you need to ask for bread and meat or bread and cheese, etc.

Digression: Turtles

Turtle, not being at this time an endangered species, is considered a delicacy. It can be enjoyed in steaks, cutlets, or fins and, as soup, clear and puree. It is served in a number of large taverns, the most famous being The Ship and Turtle Tavern, Nos. 129 and 130, Leadenhall Street.

If you are visiting anytime after 1768 it is worth making a trip to The London Tavern. It holds live turtles in enormous vats, each holding up to two tons of turtle. Instructions for keeping turtle include this advice:

Turtles will live in cellars for three months in excellent condition if kept in the same water in which they were brought to this country. To change the water is to lessen the weight and flavour of the turtle.

The usual allowance at what is called a Turtle Dinner is 6lb. live weight per head. At the Spanish Dinner in the *City of London Tavern* in 1808, four hundred guests attended and 2500lb. of turtle were consumed. If you can cadge an invitation to the Banquet at the Guildhall on

Lord Mayor's Day, you will find 250 tureens of turtle are provided.

Be aware that Mock Turtle soup, although available from mid-century, is not made of turtles - there are various recipes but expect calf's brain, oysters, onions and hard-boiled egg yolks.

Tobacco

Tobacco is not strictly speaking food but its use is widespread and it is often an accompaniment to food and drink.

Cloud; Fogus; Sot Weed; Weed	Tobacco
Mundungus	Bad quality tobacco
Blower; Gage; Organ; Steamer	Pipe
Swell Steamer	Long-stem pipe used by gentlemen
Fog; Funk	Tobacco smoke

Smoking in the Georgian period is nearly always by pipe. Cigars were manufactured in Spain in the 18th century but only become popular in Britain after the Peninsula War (1808-1814) so unless you are visiting the end of the period, do not ask for one.

Snuff is also a popular method of consuming tobacco. A *Sneezer* or *Sneezing Cofer* is a snuff box. *Snuffing* is the practice of throwing snuff into the eyes of a shopkeeper then running off with any convenient valuables.

CHAPTER SIX

Medicine and the Human Body

After all that food and drink it is possible that you are not feeling well.

You may just be *Womble-Ty-Cropt* (hung over) but food in this period is often adulterated (see previous chapter) and can cause sickness.

Hopefully you followed travel advice and packed a suitable first aid kit and some antibiotics but if you do visit a doctor you will need to be able to describe your symptoms and to do this you need to know how to describe your body.

Admittedly most of these terms will not be necessary with the better class of physician but you may find it interesting to locate a doctor used by the *Canting Crew*.

So long as you don't actually follow his advice or let him do anything to you, you should be all right.

Queer as Dick's Hatband	Feeling unwell but without any specific knowledge of a disease
Churchyard Cough	A cough that is likely to terminate in death
Crank	The falling sickness (epilepsy)
Nostrum	A medicine prepared by particular persons only, a quack medicine
Hum Durgeon	An imaginary illness
Hipped	In low spirits
Not in Plump Currant	Out of sorts
Loll Tongue	The effect of having been salivated (a mercury treatment for venereal disease)
Gravy Eyed	Blear-eyed, eyes with a running humour
Wapper Eyed	Sore eyed

The word for a 'surgeon' is 'chirurgeon'. However, with the wonderful English disdain for orthography, it is pronounced 'surgeon' so you should be all right unless you try to read the word out loud.

Digression: Surviving Medical Treatment

Medicine in Georgian London is rudimentary to say the least, although doctors and surgeons do not think so. They have a wide range of treatments, many of which are harmless, some deadly and others that might conceivably be beneficial in some cases.

Note that doctors and surgeons are completely separate professions. Indeed, before 1745 surgeons and barbers are part of the same Livery Company - The Guild of Barber-Surgeons - and it is not until 1800 that the Royal College of Surgeons is founded.

Cupping, or bleeding, is a much-used panacea, designed to let out 'bad humours'. It is mostly harmless except that there is no real concept of hygiene so if the person before you had any blood-transmittable disease you stand a chance of getting it too. Leeches, although unpleasant to contemplate, are a much safer way of removing blood. They are not, in this period, as popular as lancets.

Mercury is also regarded as having beneficial properties, particularly in the treatment of syphilis. Although there is some recognition of its long-term dangers (the phrase 'Mad as a Hatter' comes from the neurological damage caused by the mercury used in hat manufacture) it is not recognised as the dangerous neurotoxin it really is. Always check whether a medicine or pill contains mercury and avoid it if so.

Pharmacopeias of the period contain a wealth of recipes. Most are harmless (except those with the aforementioned mercury) and some provide much-needed protein for the malnourished. Snail water made, as you might expect, of crushed snails in water, is popular. Some might actually be useful.

Foxglove flowers contain digitalis, which is good for heart conditions. Willow bark contains aspirin and would therefore have had some success as an analgesic. Laudenam, opium dissolved in alcohol, is the most effective painkiller but it is addictive and dangerous in large quantities.

There are no antibiotics. If you have followed advice and taken some with you then use those for infections.

Oh yes, and there are no anaesthetics apart from large doses of alcohol or laudanum. Samuel Pepys survived a bladder stone operation in 1658 but he was lucky and the experience cannot have been a pleasant one. Avoid surgery.

Head, Hair, Face and Neck

Cannister; Costard; Crown Office; Garret; Idea Pot; Jobbernole; Jolly; Jolly Nob; Knob; Knowledge Box; Noddle; Nous Box; Pate; Poll; Sconce; Upper Storey	Head
Strommel	Hair
Dial Plate; Mug; Munns; Physig; Phyz	Face
Colquarron; Crag; Nub; Squeeze	Neck
Gutter Lane; Red Lane; Throttle; Whistle	Throat

Ears, Eyes, Mouth and Nose

Hearing Cheats; Lugs; Wattles	Ears
Glaziers; Glimms; Goggles; Lamps; Ogles; Peepers; Sees; Top Lights	Eyes
Blubber; Bone Box; Chops; Gab; Gob; Muff; Mummer; Oven	Mouth
Boltsprit; Bowsprit; Conk; Gig; Nozzle; Smeller; Trunk	Nose
Cogs; Crashing Cheats; Grinders; Ivories; Park Paling	Teeth
Clapper; Manchester; Prating Cheat; Red Rag	Tongue
Clack; Mill Clapper; Quail Pipe	Woman's tongue

Hands, Feet, Arms and Legs

Daddles; Fams; Fambles; Mauleys; Mittens; Paws	Hands
Dew Beaters	Feet
Fins; Rammers; Smiters	Arms
Gams; Pins; Shanks; Stamps; Stumps	Legs
Marrowbones	Knees

Body, Breast and Organs

Quarron; Soul Case	Body
Apple Dumpling Shop; Dairy; Diddies; Dugs; Cupid's Kettledrums	Woman's breasts
Heaver	Breast
Bellows	Lungs
Chitterlins; Puddings	Bowels
Panter	Heart
Bread Basket; Victualling Office	Stomach

Buttocks and Genitalia

Blind Cheeks; Blind Cupid; Bumfiddle; Cooler; Cracker; Double Jugs; Nancy; Nock; Pratts	Buttocks
Gaying Instrument; Hair Splitter; Pego; Plug Tail; Sugar Stick; Man Thomas; Whore Pipe	Male genitalia - penis
Tallywags; Twiddle Diddles; Whirlygigs	Male genitalia - testicles
Bottomless Pit; Miss Brown; Bun; Eve's Custom House; Fruitful Vine; Madge; Man Trap; Miss Laycock; Mother of all Saints; Muff; Notch; Tuzzy Muzzy; Water Mill	Female genitalia

The term *arse,* while not cant, is a perfectly reasonable (if impolite) word to describe the posterior. Americans should be aware that in Georgian England an ass (or *Spanish Trumpeter*) refers solely to the grey equiform animal with long ears.

Vermin

While we are on the topic of health we should mention lice. The lack of hygiene in Georgian England means that lice are extremely common and you may wish to carry something to kill them off. Their prevalence generates some colourful names and phrases.

Active Citizens; Chatts; Creepers; Gentleman's Companion; Light Troops; Live Stock; Scotch Greys	Lice
Crab Louse	A species of louse peculiar to the human body; the male is denominated a cock, the female a hen
Silver Laced	Covered in lice
Louse Trap	A small toothed comb

If someone tells you that the *Light Troops are in Full March,* expect to see a lot of lice crawling about. The *Headquarters of the Scotch Greys* refers to a head full of lice.

CHAPTER SEVEN

Some Useful Words

Some canting words are used commonly as modifiers or emphasisers of other words.

Not only will knowing these terms give you credibility but the combinatorial effect will greatly increase your vocabulary.

Useful Words: Cheat

Cheat translates broadly as thing and is used with other words to expand their meanings

Bleating Cheat	Sheep
Cackling Cheat	Chicken
Quacking Cheat	Duck
Famble Cheats	Rings or gloves (from *Fams* meaning hands)
Belly Cheat	Apron
Nubbing Cheat	The gallows (from *Nub* meaning neck)

Useful Words: Ken

Ken translates broadly as place:

Ken	House to be robbed
Ken Miller; Mill Ken	House breaker
Bowsing Ken	Alehouse
Flash Ken	Place, usually an alehouse, frequented by rogues
Cacklers Ken	Henhouse
Queer Ken	Prison
Snoozing Ken	Brothel
Stalling Ken	A fence's house or shop

Useful Words: Lay

Lay refers to a type of crime or cheat:

Dub Lay	Robbing houses by picking locks (a *Dub* is a lockpick)
Clouting Lay	Stealing handkerchiefs by picking pockets (a *Clout* is a handkerchief)
Roost Lay	Stealing chickens
Drag Lay	Waiting in the street to rob carts
Prad Lay	Cutting bags from behind horses
Toby Lay	Robbing on the highway. A *High Toby* man is a highwayman; a *Low Toby* man is a footpad

Similar terms are *Rig, Slum* and *Racket*, which are discussed in more detail in Chapter 13.

Useful Words: Fake

Fake is a general purpose verb implying some sort of action upon the object. The following examples are not exhaustive but give the general idea.

The term belongs to the later Georgian period.

Fake a Ken	Rob a house
Fake a Cull	Shoot, wound or cut a man
Fake a Cove in and out	Kill a man
Fake your Slangs	Cut your irons in order to escape from custody
Fake a Screen	Write a letter or other paper
Fake a Screw	Make a skeleton or false key
Fake a Cly	Pick a pocket

Useful Words: Mill

Mill is another 'act upon' word, like *Fake* but with implicitly more violence.

Used in regard to a person it can mean anything from a beating to murder, depending on the context.

A *Mill* can also mean a prize-fight, a popular form of entertainment throughout the Georgian period.

Prize-fights are discussed in more detail in Chapter 18.

Mill	Steal with violence
Mill a Glaze	Beat out an eye
Mill a Bleating Cheat	Kill a sheep
Mill a Ken	Rob a house
Mill Doll	Beat hemp in a bridewell or prison

Useful Words: Coming and Going

Given the occasional need for criminals to be urgently elsewhere there are a lot of expressions for running away, with varying degrees of urgency from a simple *Bing Avast* to a desperate *Pike on the Bene*.

Bing; Bing Avast; Buy a Brush; Give Leg Bail and Land Security; Nash; Rattle; Track	Go or go away
Hoof; Toddle; Troll about	Walk
Bolt; Brush; Give the Bag; Hike; Hop the Twig; Lope; Mizzle; Pike; Pike on the Bene; Rub; Scour; Scuttle; Shab Off; Sherry; Tip the Double; Whip Off	Run or run away
Play Least in Sight	To hide, keep out of the way, or make oneself scarce

Useful Miscellaneous Verbs

We are still a bit short of verbs (what my old primary school teacher used to refer to as 'doing words') so it is time to learn a few useful ones.

Bug; Bug Over; Tip	Give
Ding	Throw away
Dup	Enter or open a door
Fam	Feel or handle something
Famgrasp	Agree or make up a difference, from *Fam* meaning hand
Flash	Show or expose
Flick; Snic	Cut
Gammon	Deceive
Hanker after	Want
Nap the Bib	Cry
Nob it	Act with prudence and good judgement
Nut	Please with a small gift or flattering words
Queer	Spoil, puzzle or confound
Snite	Wipe or flap
Twig	Snap or break off
Wit	Know or understand
Snilch; Tout; Twig	To watch or observe carefully
York	Stare at

A request to *Famgrasp* (literally 'handshake') can be a good way to get out of an argument. To *Nob it* and *Nut* your adversary is also recommended.

Snilching your companions is an excellent way of learning how to behave in roguish circles but be subtle. *Yorking* will most likely cause offence.

CHAPTER EIGHT

Coffee Houses and Gaming Hells

It is time to visit a few clubs and coffee houses and get a feel for the social scene. After we have these under our belt we will make our first foray into the lower levels of society and visit a Gaming Hell.

Digression: Coffee Houses in Georgian London

With the exception of card sharpers and literary critics, you probably won't find many of the criminal classes in London's coffee houses in any organised way although, of course, criminals enjoy their coffee as much as anyone. Coffee houses are, however, a good place to meet people.

If you are interested in meeting literary and artistic men such as Henry Fielding, William Hogarth or Oliver Goldsmith, you should head for Covent Garden. *Button's* underneath the Piazza is the venue in the earlier Geor-

gian period. Around the middle of the century the lite-
rati move to Bedford's in Russell Street.

The *Grecian* is located in Deveraux Court, the Strand.
This is where the intelligentsia meet throughout most of
the 18th century. It includes such spectacular guests as
Sir Isaac Newton (scientist), Edmund Halley (astrono-
mer) and Sir Hans Sloane (whose collections formed the
basis of the British Museum and who, more importantly, introduced milk chocolate to Europe). By the
early 19th century it has been taken over by lawyers,
diminishing its interest somewhat.

To meet some politicians, head for Pall Mall. The *Co-
coa Tree* is the favourite venue of the Tories. Whigs go
to *St James*. If you must discuss politics, make sure you go
to the right one - otherwise you may find yourself tossed
rudely out into the street.

Businessmen, as always, are to be found in and
around the City. *Garraway's*, in Change Alley, is where
respectable businessmen go for their coffee. Stock jobbers and speculators, on the other hand, can be found a
few doors away at *Jonathan's*. If you are visiting in 1720,
this is a great place to witness the 'South Sea Bubble'
where stocks in the South Seas company went from
£100 to £1000 over the course of the year. The bubble
burst in August of that year resulting in a lot of people
losing a great deal of money. Also worth a visit is *Lloyd's*
at 16 Lombard Street, famous for the underwriting of
ships and their cargoes. The business moves to the Royal

Exchange in Cornhill in 1774 so a visit before this date is recommended.

If intellectual pursuits and politicians are not your thing and you want to meet some gamblers before heading to our Gaming Hell, you should make your way back to Covent Garden. Both *Will's* and *King's* are frequented by gamblers and by young bloods looking for a little excitement in their lives. The now famous *White's* is located at the rather more respectable address of 37-38 St James' Street. Although it eventually becomes one of the most exclusive London clubs, initially it is a coffee house open to all who wish to gamble away a fortune.

If you have been carousing until the small hours and desperately need caffeine, the *Finish* (also known as *Carpenter's*), in Covent Garden market opposite Russell Street, is always open. It is a good place to meet fellow revellers who are also feeling the night's excess.

The other main coffee house of interest is the *Russian* or *Brown Bear* in Bow Street, Covent Garden (almost everything happens in Covent Garden). This is a favourite coffee house for thief-takers and Bow Street runners and, as such, is unlikely to attract much custom from thieves and other rogues but it might be worth a visit, if only to identify the people you may have to run away from.

If you look around you will find various clubs and societies, meeting in Coffee Houses or Taverns. Some are whimsical, such as the Hugotontheonbiquiffinarians and the Preadamite Quacabites. Others such as the

Botherams or the Cat and Bagpipean Society (which
meets at the *Cat and Bagpipe* in Downing Street) are
simply convivial societies. There are the Hum Drums
(who meet at the *King's Head* in St John's Street) and the
Kill Care Club and societies for all tastes.

Gaming Hells

We have digressed somewhat from our original remit so it is now time to make our first expedition to the
London underworld. To start with we will go for the
Gaming Hells where any mistakes you make will be put
down to your being a visitor from the country or over-
seas, a fine target to be relieved of your money.

Georgian London is well-supplied with gambling establishments. No tour is complete without visiting one,
but it is as well to be careful. Do not expect to win any
money - you will undoubtedly be fleeced by experts.

The most famous Gaming Hells are around St James'
but this is a very upmarket area. While it makes sense
for the Hells to set up in areas where people have
money, you are likely to meet more gentlemen than
honest rogues. For a more authentic underworld experience, ask around at a disreputable tavern such as the
Queen's Head in Bow Street. They will soon set you right.

It is not the purpose of this book to teach you to play
cards or dice but before you set out, make sure you
know the following games:

Cards: *Cribbage, Loo, Faro* or *Pharoah, Picquet, Whist*
Dice: *Hazard, Novem, Passage* or *Passe-Dix*

Gamesters and Sharpers

Chub; Cub; Greenhead; Greenhorn	An inexperienced young man - an easy target
Beau Trap; Bully Trap; Cunning Man; Jack in a Box; Mace Cove; Needle Point; Nickum; Sharper; Shark; Shurk; Wheedle	Cheat or sharper
Bubble	The party cheated
Captain Sharp	A bully whose particular task is to browbeat any victims who claim they have been cheated
Cross Bite; Hunting	One who combines with a sharper to draw in a friend or other third party
Dished Up; Done Up	Ruined by gaming and extravagance
Elbow Shaker	Gamester or dice player
Gold Droppers; Money Droppers; Sweeteners	Sharpers who drop money and pretend to find it in front of their victim. They draw him into an alehouse to celebrate, then introduce gambling friends who proceed to fleece him
Lurched	Beaten at any game

Mongrel	A hanger-on among cheats
Skin	Strip a man of all his money
Vowel	A gamester who does not immediately pay his losings, is said to vowel the winner, where the acknowledgment of the debt is expressed by the letters I. O. U.
Bilk; Chouse; Fling	To cheat or trick
Taken in	Imposed on, cheated
Trapan	To inveigle, or ensnare

Be aware that sharpers often work in groups. A typical setup consists of the banker, the *Gripe* (who places bets) and the *Vincent* (the innocent victim). The gains are called *Termage*.

Card Games

Books; Broads; Devil's Books; Flats; History of the Four Kings; Child's Best Guide	Playing cards
Fore Pokers	Aces and kings
Pam	The knave of clubs
Swabbers	The ace of hearts, knave of clubs, ace and deuce of trumps at whist

Tom Bray's Bilk	Laying out ace and deuce at cribbage
Tom Brown	Twelve in hand or crib
Wibling's Witch	The four of clubs
Curse of Scotland	Nine of diamonds
Lurched	Losing a game of whist without scoring five points
Fuzz the cards	Shuffle minutely
Plant the Books	Place the cards in the pack in an unfair manner
Rout	Private card party
No face but his own	One who has no money in his pocket or no court cards in his hand.

Dice Games
Digression: How to Make False Dice

You will not, of course, be making false dice yourself, but it is worth being familiar with the techniques.

There are two main methods for altering or *Cogging* dice: loading and shaving.

Loaded dice are weighted on sides, edges or corners by inserting a small amount of some heavy metal such as gold or mercury. Particularly clever are *Tappers* which have a drop of mercury in the centre with a capillary tube leading to another reservoir on the side. The dice will roll normally until they are tapped against a hard surface at which point the mercury migrates to the side reservoir and creates the bias.

Shaved dice are biased by subtly altering their shape. If one dimension is slightly longer then the numbers at either end will roll less often. Edges and corners can be slightly rounded to make the die more likely to roll off a given side.

An additional, rather cruder, method is *Bristling* whereby a pig's bristle or similar is stuck to a corner or side. The bristle being springy, it will tend to push away from that side or corner and roll to a different number. I suspect the gull would need to be drunk and the light dim for this one to work but it is the easiest method of adding bias.

Some of the results of the biases may not be apparent without thought. For example, if your dice cannot throw a four or a three (*bard cater traes* dice) then it is impossible to roll a five or a nine with two dice. This would be particularly relevant in a game of hazard if you called a main (the number you have said will win) of one of these numbers.

A Sharper's Toolkit

The following is a list of the equipment a dice sharper or *Tat Monger* might be expected to carry. A *Bale* is a matched set of two or three dice.

A bale of bard cinque deuces	Biased against fives and twos
A bale of flat cinque deuces	Biased in favour of fives and twos

A bale of flat sice aces	Biased in favour of sixes and ones
A bale of bard cater traes	Biased against fours and threes
A bale of fulhams	Biased in favour of fours and threes
A bale of direct contraries	Dice the exact opposite to those in play so that a sharper can swap, for example, sets of high and low rollers depending on the stage of the game
A bale of langrets contrary to the ventage	As for contraries. Langrets derives from 'long' and refers to one dimension being longer than the others
A bale of gourdes, with as many highmen as lowmen for passage	As for contraries. Passage (or Passe-Dix) is a game played with three dice where the player tries to roll above or below ten, depending on whether they are currently the banker
A bale of demies	Demies are more subtly biased, only half as heavily as your standard false dice

A bale of long dice for even and odds	Contraries biased towards even or odd numbers
A bale of bristles	Dice biased by adding a pig's bristle to a corner or side

Fulham probably derives from 'full' - i.e. filled with a heavy metal to bias it. It has been suggested it relates to the village of Fulham but a visit by the author to that unoffending place has failed to detect any hive of illicit gambling activities.

Dice Terminology

Bones; St Hugh's Bones	Dice of any description
Dispatches; Dispatchers; Tats	Loaded dice
Doctors	Dice that will give only two or three results
Downhills	Dice that run low
Uphills	Dice that run high
Cog	To cheat at dice
Crabs	A losing throw to the main at hazard
Dribble	Pouring the dice out of the dice box very gently
Long Gallery	Throwing dice the full length of the table
Nick it	To win at dice
Rattle	The dice box

| Stamp | Throwing dice by striking the box hard against the table |

Beware of the man who *Dribbles* the dice - a skilled practitioner can *Cog* the dice with his little finger. Also, keep an eye out for the man *Playing Booty* - deliberately playing to lose. He is a member of the team, there to give you unwarranted confidence in your ability or luck.

Other Amusements

This is probably a good point to mention some other amusements and their related words.

Horse Racing

Daisy Cutter	A horse that does not lift up his legs sufficiently and is apt to stumble
Drummer	A horse that throws about his fore legs irregularly
Knowing Ones	Sportsmen on the turf, who from experience and an acquaintance with the jockeys, are supposed to be in the secret, that is, to know the true merits or powers of each horse

Let into the Secret	An ironic term for being cheated at horse-racing or gaming
Man of the Turf	A horse racer or jockey
Run a Crimp	To illegally influence the outcome of a race
Post; Post the Pony	Lay a bet
Run a Levant	Bet without the means to pay up if you lose

Horse racing can be fun but if a *Knowing One* puts you onto a *Sure Thing* you have probably been *Let in on a Secret* and someone is about to *Run a Crimp*. Think carefully before you *Post the Pony* or you are likely to be *Skinned*.

Cock Fighting and Bull Baiting

Cock fighting and animal baiting sports are illegal today in most countries but in the 18th century the concept of cruelty to animals was not universally accepted. Things began to change in the 19th century with the first anti-cruelty bill being introduced to parliament in 1822 and with the formation of the Society for the Prevention of Cruelty to Animals in 1824. Cock fighting and bull and bear baiting were finally outlawed in 1835.

If you are interested in seeing one of these events just ask around, but you may find your modern sensibilities are offended.

Basket	An exclamation at cock-fights, where persons refusing or unable to pay their losings are put into a basket suspended over the pit
Sparking Blows	Blows given by cocks before they close
Bull Hanker	One who enjoys bull-hanking or bull-baiting
Hank	A bull-bait

Coin Toss Games

Chouse	A game involving trying to toss your coin closest to a mark
Fly the Mags	Gamble by tossing up a halfpenny
Gray	A half-penny, or other coin, having two heads or two tails

Rural Amusements

The following are contemporary accounts of amusements to be found at country fairs.

Mumbling the Sparrow

A cruel sport frequently practiced at wakes and fairs: for a small premium, a booby, having his hands tied behind him, has the wing of a cock sparrow put into his mouth: with this hold, without any other assistance than the motion of his lips, he is to get the sparrow's head into his mouth: on attempting to do it, the bird defends itself surprisingly, frequently pecking the mumbler till his lips are covered with blood, and he is obliged to desist.

Tup Running

A rural sport practiced at wakes and fairs in Derbyshire; a ram, whose tail is well soaped and greased, is turned out to the multitude; any one that can take him by the tail, and hold him fast, is to have him for his own.

Related Terms

All Holiday at Peckham	It is all over for a business or person
Beaten All Hollow	No chance of winning
Within Ames Ace	Nearly, very near
Blocked at Both Ends	Finished
Bobbed	Cheated, tricked, disappointed

CHAPTER NINE

Honest Work (and Shopping)

Not all the citizens of London are criminals. Many pursue perfectly or, in the cases of lawyers and stock jobbers, imperfectly innocent occupations. Rogues have their own (often derisory) terms for these people.

Honest Work

Oddly enough, there are very few cant terms for honest work.

Strap	To work
Work for a Dead Horse	To work for wages already paid

Lawyers

Lawyers are held in no higher regard than they are today. Given that the lower orders of criminals are likely to be able only to afford cheap lawyers, their cynicism is not surprising. As an example, the name for a shark is a *Sea Lawyer.*

Black Box; Green Bag; Jet; Latitat; Split-Cause	Lawyer
Cursitor; Limb of the Law; Newgate Solicitor; Petty Fogger	Poor quality lawyer
Ambidexter	A lawyer who takes fees from both the plaintiff and the defendant
Puzzle-cause	Lawyer with a confused understanding

Entertainers

Brother of the String; Crowd; Crowdero; Gut Scraper; Scraper; Tormentor of Catgut	Fiddler
Sheepskin Fiddler; Tormentor of Sheepskin	Drummer
Rump and Kidney Men	Fiddlers that play at feasts, fairs, weddings etc. and live chiefly on the remnants of victuals
Solo Player	A miserable performer on any instrument, who always plays alone, because no one will stay in the room to hear him

Raree Show Men	Men who give puppet shows in the portable boxes they carry on their backs
Faytors	Fortune tellers
Faulkner	A tumbler, juggler or shower of tricks
Flying Stationers	Ballad-singers and hawkers of penny histories
Calf-skin Fiddle	Drum
Dutch Feast	A party where the entertainer gets drunk before the guests

Teachers and Tutors

Terms such as *Flaybottomist* for schoolmaster suggest that the strongest memories of schooling consisted of bending over for the birch rod. One might hope that a little grammar was also acquired, however painfully.

Bear Leader	Travelling tutor
Pupil Monger	University tutor
Bum Brusher; Flaybottomist; Syntax; Tickle Tail	Schoolmaster
Caper Merchant; Hop Merchant; Kit	Dancing master

The term *Kit* for dancing master refers to his kit or cittern, a small fiddle, which dancing-masters always carry about with them, to play for their pupils.

Servants

Abigail	Lady's maid
Bone Picker; Catch Fart; Fart Catcher; Skip Kennel	Footman
Mopsqueezer; Nan	Female servant
Pantler	Butler

Other Professions

Bang Straw	Farm worker
Carrion Hunter; Cold Cook; Death Hunter	Undertaker
Clod Hopper	Ploughman or country farmer
Christian Pony	Chairman
Daisy Kickers	Ostlers at great inns
Deuseaville Stampers	Country carriers
Dub at a Knapping Jigger	Collector of tolls at a turn-pike gate
Gold Finder; Nightman; Tom Turdman	Night-soil man
Horse Coser; Jingler	Dealer in horses
Flue Faker; Lily White	Chimney sweep
Little Clergyman; Minor Clergy	Chimney sweep's boy
Running Stationers	Hawkers of newspapers, trials and dying speeches
Stock jobbers	Disreputable stock dealers who buy and sell without necessarily having the funds to meet losses

Tally Man	Man who rents clothes to women by the week, month or year
Translator	Seller of old and repaired shoes
Whow Ball	A milk-maid: from their frequent use of the word whow, to make the cow stand still in milking
Window Peeper	Collector of window tax
Yelper	Town crier
Glim Jack; Moon Curser	Link boy (torch bearer)
Rum Glimmer	Chief link boy
Skip Jack	Boy who rides for dealers at horse sales

Shopping

Shopkeepers are not, of course, immune to roguish practice so keep a look out for any of the following crimes.

Avoir du Pois Lay	Stealing brass weights off the counters of shops
Curbing Lay	Hooking goods out of windows
Dobin Rig	Stealing ribbands from haberdashers early in the morning or late at night; generally practiced by women disguised as maid servants
Fam Lay	Going into a goldsmith's shop, under pretence of buying a wedding ring, and palming one or two, by daubing the hand with some viscous matter
Order Racket	Obtaining goods from a shopkeeper, by means of a forged order or false pretence
Running Smobble	Snatching goods off a counter, and throwing them to an accomplice, who *Brushes Off* with them

Shopkeepers and Tradesmen

Burn Crust; Master of the Rolls	Baker
Bug Hunter	Upholsterer
Nob Thatcher; Skull Thatcher	Peruke (wig) maker
Botch; Cucumber; Knight of the Shears; Knight of the Thimble or Needle; Linen Armourer; Prick-louse; Shred; Snip; Stay-tape; Stitch; Winter Cricket	Tailor
Maggot Boiler	Tallow chandler
Chicken Butcher; Strangle Goose	Poulterer
Ambassador of Morocco; Crispin; Gentle Crafts-man; Snob	Shoemaker
Mite	Cheesemonger
Nit Squeezer	Hairdresser
Quarrel Picker	Glazier
Barker; Salesman's Dog	Salesman's servant who walks before the shop, to invite customers
Mix Metal; Witcher Cully	Silversmith
Ridge Cully	Goldsmith
Smear	Plasterer
Smug; Split Iron	Blacksmith
Split Fig	Grocer

Shopping for Clothes

If you got carried away in the Gaming Hell and inadvertently gambled away your coat you will need a new one. Even if this is not the case you should get yourself properly kitted out.

You should dress to be *All the Crack*, a regular *Pink of the Fashion*. Your *Kicks* (breeches) must be *Rum* not *Queer*, your *Vampers* (stockings) made of silk and your *Shap* (hat) made of beaver fur.

Try Mr John Newcomb of 103 Pall Mall for your boots. I found Griffin and Son at 123 New Bond Street to be an excellent for gloves, hats and general haberdashery but there is no need to take my advice here. Just look around. London is teeming with clothing outlets.

The Crack; All the Crack	The fashionable theme, the go
Well-rigged Frigate	Well-dressed woman
Beau-Nasty	A slovenly fop; one finely dressed, but dirty
Bartholomew Baby; Bartholomew Doll	A person dressed up in a tawdry manner, like the dolls or babies sold at Bartholomew fair
Dapper Fellow	A smart, well-made, little man
Jemmy Fellow	A smart spruce man
Pink of the Fashion	The top of the mode (both men and women)

Coats and Cloaks

Calle; Cardinal; Caster; Togemans; Vinegar	Cloak
Mish Topper; Tog; Toge	Coat
Upper Benjamin; Upper Toge	Great coat

Shoes and Stockings

Beaters; Pipes	Boots
Crab Shells; Flyers; Hopper-Dockers; Stampers	Shoes
Drawers; Stock Drawers; Vampers	Stockings
Queer Drawers	Yarn or worsted stockings
Rum Drawers	Silk stockings

Fallen stitches in stockings are called *Louse Ladders.*

Breeches, Shirts and Petticoats

Farting Crackers; Hams; Inexpressibles; Kicks; Kickseys; Small Clothes	Breeches
Queer Kicks	Old and tattered breeches
Rum Kicks	Breeches with gold and silver brocade or lace
Camesa; Commission; Flesh-Bag; Smish	Shirt
Buntlings	Petticoats
Jacobites; Numms	Sham collars to hide dirty shirts

Accessories

Clout; Wiper	Handkerchief
Fogle; India Wipe; Rum Clout; Rum Wiper	Silk handkerchief
Kent; Specked Wiper	Coloured handkerchief
Belcher	Red silk handkerchief intermixed with yellow and black
Barnacles	Spectacles
Belly Cheat; Bunt	Apron
Knuckle-Dabs; Knuckle-Confounders	Ruffles at the wrist
Bung; Haddock; Skin	Purse
Cly; Sack; Sock	Pocket
Garret; Rough Fam	Waistcoat or fob pocket
Hoxter	Inside coat pocket
Salt Box Cly	Outside coat pocket covered in a flap

Hats

Castor; Kelp; Nab Cheat; Shallow; Shappo; Shap	Hat
Penthouse Nab	Large, broad-brimmed hat
Beaver; Rum Nab	Good quality hat of beaver fur
Queer Nab	Hat made of felt or cloth
Commode; Rum Topping	Good quality women's hat

Digression: Wigs

The extent to which you encounter wigs depends very much on which part of the Georgian period you are visiting. Wigs (also known as perukes or periwigs) were popularised in France in the 17th century by Kings Louis XIII and XIV. They arrived in England in 1660 with the restoration of King Charles II. The fashion then was for very long wigs falling well past the shoulders.

The *perruquier* or peruke maker (*Nob Thatcher* or *Skull Thatcher* to the vulgar) was a skilled craftsman. Throughout most of the 18th century he was in high demand but by the end he was endangered species. Fashions had changed and wigs were no longer in demand.

In the Georgian period you will find long wigs at the beginning of the period but they gradually become shorter until they are like the short wigs worn by barristers today. Wigs are powdered with a finely ground starch scented with orange flower or lavender, giving them the distinctive white or off-white colour. Women's hair powder is grey or grey-blue. By the 1780s, young men at the vanguard of fashion are powdering their own hair in preference to wearing a wig. By 1790 it is only the older generation who wear wigs and powder. In 1795 the British government levied a tax on hair powder, which pretty much killed off any remaining interest in wigs or hair powdering.

Wigs were far less common among women although many wore hair extensions, particularly during the 1770s when the enormous *pouf* style become popular.

If you are in the wig-wearing period and want the full low-life experience, you can *Dip* for a wig. Visit Middle Row, Holborn, where you will find wigs of different sorts put into a close-stool box. For three-pence, you can dip, or thrust in a hand, and blindly take out a wig. If you don't like it you can pay another three half-pence to try again. You will be lucky to find anything of any quality but you will have the fun of owning a probably stolen object.

Flash; Jazey; Periwinkle; Strum	Wig
Caxon; Queer Flash; Scandalous	Old, weather-beaten wig
Rum Flash; Rum Strum	Long haired wig
Cauliflower	A large white wig, such as is commonly worn by the clergy
Gooseberry Wig	A large frizzled wig
Owl in an Ivy Bush	A person with a large frizzled wig, or a woman with hair dressed a-la-blowze

A man wearing a wig is known as a *Wigannowns* or *Wigsby*.

CHAPTER TEN

People

We covered the basic words for parts of the body in Chapter 6 but there are a lot of descriptive terms we have not touched. You will often hear people (including Rogues) described in these terms so you need to be aware of them.

Head and Face

Bleached Mort	A fair-complexioned woman
Bracket Faced	Ugly, hard featured
Bran Faced	Freckled
Brandy Faced; Ruby Faced	Red faced
Carbuncle, Corny Faced	Red, pimpled face
Chitty Faced	Baby faced
Friday Face	Dismal countenance
Frosty Faced; Stub Faced	Marked with smallpox
Hatchett Faced; Lockeram Jawed; Lanthorn Jawed	Long, thin face
Muzzle	A beard, (usually) long and nasty
Bacon Faced; Platter Faced	Broad faced

Blubber Faced	Large flaccid cheeks, hanging like the fat or blubber of a whale
Rosy Gills; Smock Faced	Fair faced
Weasel Faced	Thin, meagre faced
Beetle Browed	Thick, projecting eyebrows
Gimblet Eyed; Moon Eyed; Swivel Eyed	Squinting
Gooseberry Eyed	One with dull grey eyes, like boiled gooseberries
Fed with a Fire Shovel; Sparrow Mouthed	Wide-mouthed
Malmsey Nose	Red nose
Light House	Red fiery nose
Pug or Stub Nose	Short nose turned up at the end
Carrot Pate; Ginger Hackled; Poison Pate	Red haired
Turnip Pate	White or fair haired

Body and Limbs

Duck Legs	Short legs
Crook Shanks	A man with bandy legs
Spider Shanks; Spindle Shanks; Trap Sticks	Thin legs
Long Shanks	Long legged
Baker-Kneed	One whose knees knock together in walking, as if kneading dough

Chicken-Hammed	Persons whose legs and thighs are bent or arched outwards
Chicken-Breasted	A woman with small breasts
Corporation	A large belly
Gotch Gutted	Pot bellied
Herring Gutted	Thin
Wide in the Boughs	With large hips and posteriors
Bushel Bubby	A full breasted woman
Crump-Backed	Hump-backed

More Physical Descriptions

Chit; Dandyprat; Jack Sprat; Kinchin Cove; Minikin; Shrimp; Tom Thumb	A small person
Duke of Limbs; Mackerel Back	A very tall, lank person
Banging; Bull Calf; Two-Handed; Thumping; Whapper	A large person
Chopping	Lusty
Crummy; Gundiguts	Fat, fleshy
Fubsey	Plump
Groper	Blind man
Squeeze Crab	A sour-looking, shrivelled, diminutive person

Clumsy, Stupid and Foolish

There are an enormous number of ways to insult someone by calling them stupid or foolish. Do not try to learn them all - just pick a dozen or so of your favourites.

Cow Handed; Clumpish; Clunch	Clumsy
Gudgeon	One easily imposed on
Addle Pate; Beetle-Headed; Ben; Benish; Bird Witted; Bottle Headed; Buffle Headed; Cake; Chuckle Head; Cod's Head; Cony; Goose Cap; Jack Adams; Jingle Brains; Mutton Headed; Nick Ninny; Nigit; Nigmenog; Ninnyhammer; Nocky; Noddy; Nokes; Numb-skull; Paper Skull; Pig Widgeon; Pudding Head; Sapskull; Sir Quibble Queer; Tom Cony; Totty Headed; Woolley Crown	Stupid or foolish
Chaw Bacon; Clouted Shoon; Hick; High Shoon; Hob; Hobnail; Hodge; Joskin; Milestone; Put	Country bumpkin
Dicked in the Nob	Silly or crazed

Vain and Cowardly

Coxcomb	A fop, or vain self-conceited fellow
Cracking	Boasting
Purse Proud	One that is vain of his riches
Stiff-rumped	Proud, stately
Uppish	Testy, apt to take offence
Pisses more than he Drinks	One who boasts without reason
Chicken-Hearted; Hen-Hearted	Fearful, cowardly
White-Livered	Cowardly, malicious

Clever and Sly

Clinker; Dry Boots; Fox; Whipster	Cunning or crafty man
Fly; Leary	Vigilant, suspicious - not easily duped
Nacky	Ingenious
Shuffler; Shuffling Fellow	A slippery, shifting fellow
Sly Boots	A cunning fellow under the mask of simplicity
Cunning Shaver	A subtle, smart fellow
Tongue Pad	A smooth, glib-tongued, insinuating fellow

Speech, Scolding and Abuse

Chivey; Huff; Maundering Broth	Reprove or scold
Comb the Hair; Ring a Peal	To scold - terms chiefly applied to women
Crack; Crow	Brag, boast or triumph
Foreman of the Jury	One that engrosses all the talk to himself
Fustian	Bombastic language
Gum	Abusive language
Juniper Lecture	A round scolding bout
Jobation	A reproof
Jaw	Speech, discourse
Jaw-me-dead	A talkative person
Snoach	To speak through the nose, to snuffle
Termagant	An outrageous scold (female)

Miscellaneous Terms

Blue Devils	Low spirits
Crab Lanthorn	A peevish fellow
Cagged; Moped	Melancholy
Clean; Dab	Expert, clever
Close-Fisted	Covetous or stingy
Muckworm; Nip Cheese	A miser
Take Snuff	To be offended
Tweaguey	Peevish, passionate
Twiddle Poop	An effeminate looking fellow

CHAPTER ELEVEN

Religion and Society

Religion in the Georgian period meant Christianity.

There was Judaism, of course, but the Jewish population in Britain was not large (perhaps 20,000 at the end of the 18th century) although they were well represented among the merchants and brokers on the Royal Exchange. In our London underworld they are mostly viewed as moneylenders and pawnbrokers, a matter of function not religion.

There were a few Muslims, mostly lascars - sailors recruited from India by the British East India Company who had subsequently settled in port towns. Some African ex-slaves would have practiced Vodun or Voodoo. Possibly a few Druids still lurked in the wilds of Anglesey but Christianity was the norm.

A church is an *Autem* and the congregation is the *Hums*. The pulpit is the *Hum Box* or the *Prattling Box*.

Autem Bawler; Autem Jet; Black Coat; Devil Catcher; Devil Driver; Levite; Parish Bull; Prunella; Pudding Sleeves; Snub Devil; Soul Doctor; Soul Driver; Tickle Text	General term for parson
Finger Post	A parson: so called, because he points out a way to others which he has never been on himself and probably never will i.e. the way to heaven
Gluepot	A parson: from joining men and women together in matrimony
Old Dog at Common Prayer	A poor hackney parson that can read but not preach well
One in Ten	A parson: an allusion to tithes
Postillion of the Gospel	A parson who hurries over the service
Spoil Pudding	A parson who preaches long sermons, keeping his congregation in church till the puddings are overdone
Chop the Whiners	Hurry over the prayers

Turnpike Man	A parson; because the clergy collect their tolls at our entrance into and exit from the world
Ungrateful Man	A parson, who at least once a week abuses his best benefactor, i.e. the devil
Black Fly	The greatest drawback on the farmer is the black fly, i.e. the parson who takes a tithe of the harvest
Cushion Duster; Cushion Thumper	A parson; many of whom in the fury of their eloquence, heartily belabour their cushions
Crow Fair	A visitation of the clergy
Parson's Journeyman	Curate
Amen Curler; Canticle; Chuck Farthing; Solfa	Parish clerk
Nose Gent	Nun
Chop Churches	Simoniacal dealers in livings, or other ecclesiastical preferments
Black Spy; Old Harry	The Devil

Digression: Dissenters

The Established Church of England dozed its way through the long eighteenth century with an indolently tolerant latitudinarianism, but outside its quiet churchyards things were very different.

For anyone actually interested in God it was necessary to search elsewhere.

Dissenters - believers who did not follow the established dogma - really got going during the late 16th and 17th centuries including (alphabetically) Adamites, Anabaptists, Barrowists, Behmenists, Brownists, Diggers, Enthusiasts, Familists, Fifth Monarchists, Grindletonians, Muggletonians, Puritans, Philadelphians, Ranters, Sabbatarians, Seekers and Socinians.

In the 18th century John Wesley, a self-described Anglican, preached his fiery message throughout the country, resulting in various Methodist and Wesleyan offshoots.

There were Presbyterians of different flavours, Quakers and Unitarians, but they all had one thing in common - they could not hold public office and did not have access to the established universities of Oxford and Cambridge. It was this last that caused a quiet revolution. Dissenters formed their own schools and Universities, their standards often higher than the established institutions.

I have strayed somewhat from my remit of Thieves' Cant, and the effect of religious dissent on Georgian society is a topic too large to address here. Suffice it to say that Dissenters were visible and had a reputation for noise and enthusiasm totally lacking in the established church.

Autem Cackler; Autem Prickear	Dissenter
Mess John	Scotch Presbyterian teacher or parson
Tub Thumper	Presbyterian parson
Aminadab; Autem Quaver	Quaker
New Light; Whitfieldite	Methodist
Autem Dipper	Anabaptist
Autem Cackletub; Cockpit; Steeple House	Conventicle or meeting house for Dissenters
Autem Quaver Tub	Quaker meeting house

Digression: Catholics and the Stuart Succession

The 'third leg' of British Christianity in this period was Catholicism. Being a Dissenter could be difficult but being a Catholic was potentially fatal.

Catholicism, at least until the middle of the 18th century, was very tied up with politics.

The Catholic Stuart monarchs had been replaced with the Hanoverians but not everyone agreed with the decision. James II attempted to regain the throne by landing with French troops in Ireland but was defeated at the Battle of the Boyne.

In 1715, his son James Stuart (the Old Pretender) attempted to regain the throne with no more success.

In 1745, the Stuarts tried again, this time with Bonnie Prince Charlie (the Young Pretender). After landing in Scotland with virtually no resources, he gathered together an army - mostly from the highland clans - and successfully marched south as far as Derby until the Lairds lost faith and they all marched back to Scotland again.

The rebellion came to a bloody end at the battle of Culloden Moor and although the Prince escaped, that was the last effective chance the Stuarts had of regaining the throne.

The treason act of 1351, which still applied, made it treason to give aid and comfort to the King's enemies in his Realm or elsewhere.

If you start with the premise that Catholics are enemies of the realm then it is not too much of a stretch to see the mere act of being a Catholic priest being the same as treason. With the Stuarts added to the mix it all got very unpleasant.

The position of Catholics was much improved by the Catholic Relief Act of 1778 which allowed them to again own property, inherit land and join the armed forces, provided they rejected the Stuart succession and the civil jurisdiction of the Pope.

The Relief Act of 1829 put the whole thing to bed (legally, at any rate) and allowed, among other things, Catholics to become members of Parliament.

Given the upheavals in the middle of the 18th century it is perhaps a little ironic that the music for 'Rule Britannia' was written by the Catholic Thomas Arne in 1740.

Society

This book will not teach you how to function among the *Swells* (although see the Digression on *Spruce Prigs* in Chapter 17). There are nevertheless a few associated terms it is worth knowing.

Glaver	To fawn and flatter
Gorger	A gentleman
Hanger On	A dependant
Make a Leg	To bow
Mushroom	A person or family suddenly raised to riches and eminence
None-Such	One that is unequalled: often applied ironically
Pink of the Fashion	Top of the mode
Tuft Hunter	A parasite, one who courts the acquaintance of nobility, whose caps are adorned with a gold tuft
Toad Eater	A poor female relation or reduced gentlewoman in a great family
Upstarts	Persons lately raised to honours and riches from mean stations
Lollop	To lean with one's elbows on a table
The Crack; All the Crack; The Go	The fashionable trend, the mode

The term *Toad Eater* derives from a mountebank's servant, on whom all experiments used to be made in public by the doctor, his master; among which was the eating of toads, formerly supposed poisonous. Swallowing toads is here figuratively meant for swallowing or putting up with insults.

CHAPTER TWELVE

The Ancient Orders of Rogues

There are reported to be twenty-three orders of the canting crew - fourteen male and nine female.

The list was compiled in the 16th century but continues through the 18th and so has some relevance.

There are many rogues not in this list whom we will come to shortly.

I have left the contemporary descriptions of the categories mostly intact to give something of their flavour.

Major Orders of Rogues

Upright Men

The Upright-man is the chief man of a crew - the vilest, stoutest rogue in the pack. He is reported to have a droit du seigneur with the Dells, who afterwards are used in common among the whole fraternity.

He carries a short truncheon in his hand, which he calls his Filchman, and is entitled to a greater share of any proceeds of villainy.

Abrams or Toms of Bedlam

Shabby beggars, patched and tricked up with ribbons, red-tape, fox-tails, rags of various colours; pretending to be insane to palliate their thefts of poultry, linen, etc.

Bawdy Baskets

Pedlars, usually women, who sell obscene books, pins, tape, etc. but live more by pilfering and stealing.

Counterfeit Cranks

Beggars who pretend to have the falling sickness (epilepsy).

They wear dirty clothes and carry soap so that they can use it to foam at the mouth.

Demanders for Glimmer or Fire

Beggars who pretend to have suffered losses by fire, carrying counterfeit passes.

This role was often undertaken by women.

Drommerers

Rogues, pretending to have had their tongues cut out, or to be born dumb and deaf, who artificially turn the tip of their tongues into their throat, and with a stick make it bleed.

Fraters

Vagabonds who beg with sham patents, or briefs, for hospitals, fires, inundations, etc.

Fresh Water Mariners, or Whip Jackets

Counterfeit mariners begging with false passes, pretending shipwrecks, great losses at sea, narrow escapes, etc. telling dismal stories, having learnt tar-terms on purpose.

Hookers or Anglers

Petty thieves, who have a stick with a hook at the end, wherewith they pluck things out of windows, grates, etc.

Jarkmen, or Patricoes

Those who make counterfeit licences and passes, and are well paid by the other beggars for their pains.

Patricoes were poor clergymen trying to earn a bit on the side. Particularly early on, they were one of the few groups with the literacy required to forge documents. The word derives from *Pater Cove* - a general term for a clergyman.

Palliardes

Those whose fathers were clapperdogeons, or beggars born, and who themselves follow the same trade: the female sort beg with a number of children, borrowing them, if they have not a sufficient number of their own, and making them cry by pinching in order to excite charity; the males make artificial sores on different parts of their bodies, to move compassion.

Priggers of Prancers

Horse-stealers, who carry a bridle in their pockets, and a small pad saddle in their breeches.

Rufflers

Notorious rogues, who, under pretence of being maimed soldiers or seamen, implore the charity of well disposed persons, and fail not to watch opportunities either to steal, break open houses, or even commit murder.

Drunken Tinkers

These never go without their Doxies, and if their women have anything about them, as apparel or linen, that is worth the selling, they lay the same to gage, or sell it outright for bene bouse at their bousing ken.

Swaddlers, or Pedlars

Rogues, who, not content to rob and plunder, beat and barbarously abuse, and often murder.

Rogues

A Rogue is neither so stout nor hardy as the upright man.

These are the 'rank and file' of the profession.

Wild Rogues

Rogues trained up to stealing from their cradles; such as are trained up from children to Nim golden or silver buttons from coats, to creep in at cellar and shop-windows, and to slip in at doors behind people.

Women and Children

There are also categories of women and children that are defined in terms of men or (in the case of children) their parents.

Autem Morts

Female rogues who were married in a church (Autem) who use their children to steal from houses.

Delles

Female rogues who are still virgins. Quite often they are wild rogues.

Doxies

Female rogues whose virginity was taken by the Upright Man.

Walking Morts

Who, pretending to be widows, often travel the countries, making laces upon yews, beggars-tape, etc. Are light-fingered, subtle, hypocritical, cruel, and often dangerous to meet, especially when a Ruffler is with them.

Kinching Morts

Girls of a year or two old, whom the morts (their mothers) carry at their backs in Slates (sheets) and if they have no children of their own, they borrow or steal them from others.

Kinching Coves

Little children whose parents are dead, having been beggars; also young lads running from their masters, who are first taught canting, then thieving.

CHAPTER THIRTEEN

Crime

Unsurprisingly, there are a lot of canting terms for crime but I recommend nevertheless that you study this chapter carefully.

A knowledge of the terminology of crime will go a long way to establishing your credentials.

General Terms for Crime

Cloy; Do; Filch; File; Fleece; Give it to; Heave; Knap; Make; Nail; Nim; Nip; Pick; Pinch; Shake; Snabble; Snaffle; Speak with; Strike; Win	Steal
Click	Snatch
Crib; Weed	To steal part of something such as a few banknotes out of a roll
Mill	Steal with violence

Proceeds of Crime

Spilt	A small reward or gift
Whack	A share of a booty obtained by fraud
Well	To divide unfairly

Rigs, Lays, Slums and Rackets

Rigs, Lays, Slums and *Rackets* all refer to particular types of crime. The term *Racket* belongs to the later Georgian period. The terms *Game* and *Suit* can also be used if preferred.

We encountered some of these terms in earlier chapters but I have repeated them here as a reminder.

Area Sneak; Area Slum	The practice of slipping unperceived down the areas of private houses, and robbing the lower apartments of plate or other articles
Avoir du Pois Lay	Stealing brass weights off the counters of shops
Black Spice Racket	Robbing chimney sweepers of their soot bag and soot
Bleating Rig	Sheep stealing
Cat and Kitten Rig	The petty game of stealing pewter quart and pint pots from public-houses

Chiving Lay	Cutting the braces of coaches behind, on which the coachman quitting the box, an accomplice robs the boot; also cutting the back of the coach to steal wigs
Clouting Lay	Picking pockets of hand-kerchiefs
Crack Lay	House-breaking
Curbing Lay	Hooking goods out of windows: the *Curber* is the thief, the *Curb* the hook
Dobin Rig	Stealing ribbands from haberdashers early in the morning or late at night; generally practiced by women in the guise of maid servants
Drag Lay	Waiting in the streets to rob carts or wagons
Dub Lay; Going upon the Dub	Robbing houses by picking locks
Fam Lay	Going into a goldsmith's shop, under pretence of buying a wedding ring, and palming one or two, by daubing the hand with some viscous matter

Fawney Rig	Dropping a brass ring, double gilt, which the rogue picks up before the party meant to be cheated, and to whom he sells it for less than its supposed, and ten times more than its real, value
Kid Lay	Defrauding apprentices, or errand-boys, by prevailing on them to execute some trifling message, pretending to take care of their parcels till they come back
Konoblin Rig	Stealing large pieces of coal from coal sheds
Letter Racket	Going to respectable houses with a letter or statement, detailing some case of extreme distress, such as shipwreck, sufferings by fire, etc.
Lodging Slum	The practice of hiring furnished lodgings, and stripping them of the plate, linen, and other valuables
Lowing Rig	Stealing oxen or cows
Mill Lay	Robbing houses by breaking in the doors
Noisy Dog Racket	Stealing brass knockers from doors

Order Racket	Obtaining goods from a shopkeeper, via a forged order or false pretence.
Palming Racket	Secreting money in the palm of the hand
Peter Lay	Petty thefts; such as cutting bags from behind coaches, breaking shop glasses, etc.
Prad Lay	Cutting bags from behind horses
Roost Lay	Stealing poultry
Shutter Racket	The practice of robbing houses, or shops, by boring a hole in the window shutter, and taking out a pane of glass
Star Lay	Breaking shop-windows, and stealing some article
Smug Lay	Persons who pretend to be smugglers of lace and valuable articles; they borrow money against these goods which subsequently prove to be worthless
Sword Racket	To enlist in different regiments and, on receiving the bounty, to desert
Toby Lay	Robbery on the highway
Tolliban Rig	A cheat carried on by a woman, pretending to be a dumb and deaf conjuror

Tools of the Trade

Locksmith's Daughter	Key
Charm; Dub; Screw	Lockpick or false key
Bess; Betty	A small instrument used by house-breakers to force open doors
Curb	A hook used to steal items from windows
Darky; Glim; Guy	Dark lantern
Ginny; Jenny	An instrument to lift up a grate
James; Jemmy; Jemmy Rook	Crowbar
Round About	An instrument for cutting a circle big enough to insert an arm in a door or shutter
Buffer's Nab; Jark; Prancer's Head	Seal used when forging documents
Nipps	Shears for clipping money
Skew	Beggar's wooden bowl
Filch; Filel	Beggar's staff, with an iron hook at the end, to pluck clothes from an hedge, or anything out of a casement
Campaign Coat	The ragged coat, worn by beggars and gypsies, in order to move compassion

Arrest and Trial

Being arrested and tried in court is one of the occupational hazards of being a rogue. There is a range of punishments available to the Magistrate or Judge, from a flogging or a session in the pillory (or both) right the way up to hanging or transportation to the colonies.

There are surprisingly few terms directly associated with trials - nearly all are concerned with the punishments receivable as an outcome. The most feared outcome - a death sentence - is referred to graphically as *Cramp Words*.

Digression: Law and Justice in Georgian England

Laws could be draconian and their application unfair but there was a rough justice to be had in the English courts. The poor were treated much more harshly than the rich (*plus ça change*) but arrest did not lead automatically to conviction nor conviction to harsh punishment.

Courts are, after all, run by people and the people of Georgian England had a strong sense of natural justice, which is not necessarily the same as the law.

The number of capital offenses during the period increased drastically but the number of people actually executed decreased steadily.

Stolen goods were commonly undervalued by the court in order to reduce the hanging offence of grand larceny to petty theft.

People were allowed to speak up for the convicted and a plea for clemency by a Master for his employees or poor relations was often heeded.

Also, pregnant women could make a *Belly Plea* of pregnancy, delaying execution of their sentence until after the child was born and giving the chance to obtain a reprieve. Reportedly, every prison had *Child Getters*, who would get women pregnant for the purpose.

The occasional humanity of the courts is shown in an account of the trial of a woman convicted of stealing a piece of meat in order to feed her children.

The sympathetic judge sentenced her to a token fine of one shilling, which itself was paid for by a whip-round of the jury.

A large number of cases were thrown out through lack of evidence, regardless of the importance of the plaintiff.

Nevertheless laws and punishments were harsh by modern standards.

About 200 people per year were hanged. Approximately three times that number were sentenced to execution but the courts also liked to try and shock people into better behaviour by delivering a reprieve at the gallows.

There are several unfortunate cases of the reprieve arriving too late because the server was caught up in the crowds there to watch the hanging.

Digression: Thief-takers and Bow Street Runners

The first patrols of the London Metropolitan Police Force were not on the streets until 29th September 1829. In the early Georgian period, such policing as there was was done by private individuals known as 'Thief-takers' who would track down miscreants for a fee.

Thief-taking could be highly remunerative - the reward for a capital crime was £40, which was a large amount of money.

It was not unknown for thief-takers to overlook minor crimes until the criminal *Weighed Forty*, that is, had committed a capital offense, at which point the reward became worth the effort.

Corruption, unsurprisingly, was rife. Thief-takers like Jonathan Wild (executed in 1725) were also criminals, running both sides of the game and having their rivals hanged for a rich reward.

Unhappy with this state of affairs, magistrate and author Henry Fielding formed the 'Bow Street Runners' who worked out of the Bow Street Magistrates' office.

They served writs and arrested criminals on behalf of the magistrates and were paid out of the public purse.

Although by no means incorruptible and not always paid, the Runners did contribute to order in the city and held the line until they were finally disbanded in 1839.

Cry Beef	Give the alarm
Blood Money	The reward given by the legislature on the conviction of highwaymen, burglars, etc.
Buck Bail	Bail given by a sharper for one of the gang
Bum	Arrest a debtor
Body Snatchers	Bum bailiffs
Civility Money	A reward claimed by bailiffs for executing their office with civility
Janizaries; Myrmidons	Bailiffs, their setters, and followers
Bone; Roast; Touch	Arrest
Boning the Fence	Finding where (stolen) goods are concealed and seizing them
Romboyled	Sought after with a warrant
Served	Found guilty and ordered to be punished or transported
Ware Hawk	A warning that a bailiff is approaching

CHAPTER FOURTEEN

Rogues in the Gutters

Everywhere you go in London you will encounter beggars. It can be hard to distinguish the professionals from those in desperate need. The division between rich and poor is huge and at the bottom of the heap it can be a struggle to stay alive.

Digression: Poverty in Georgian London

Anyone who is outraged by incompetent Chief Executive Officers earning fifty times as much as their (soon to be redundant) employees should have their blood pressure checked before visiting Georgian London. In that *laissez faire* cauldron of capitalism differences could be far greater. As an extreme example, at the time that a Ship's Boy earned £2 10s a year, the annual salary of the First Commissioner to the Admiralty was £3,000.

More reasonably, where a successful merchant might clear £400 - £600 in a year, a teacher might earn £15.

Unskilled labourers could earn 9d per day but only on those days when they were in good health and there was work available. Seasonal workers, such as agricultural labourers, were particularly hard hit as they might have half a year when they had no income. The trickle of labourers migrating to the city at the beginning of the Georgian period became a torrent as the industrial revolution took off. Work in the factories might be hard and dangerous but it paid enough to keep you alive. The population of London more than trebled between 1714 and 1830 from a base of half a million people.

Not everyone could find gainful employment. The sick and injured, single women and children were the worst hit. Even if there were work, a child would only earn 3d to 6d for a long day's labour. A silk handkerchief cost 1s, so stealing just one of these was, once you had taken the fence's cut into account, the equivalent of a day's work. The high level of crime is not surprising.

Yet many people still remained reasonably honest (see Chapter 9 for more details). In the 1730s it was reckoned that you could just raise a family of four on four shillings a week: 1s 6d for the rent of two rooms (in a run-down area) and the rest on food and fuel. However, this doesn't include clothing so it is probably unrealistic. Still, if you could scrape together 5 shillings a week you could probably survive. The aforementioned teacher, therefore, could just about raise a family if nothing went wrong.

So, with reasonable luck and good health you could survive in genteel poverty. It might be tough but at least you didn't run the risk of being hanged.

If neither of these appealed to you, you could try begging. Georgian Londoners are surprisingly charitable and you had a good chance of making a living, particularly if you could extract some sympathy.

For many, begging was what you did to get you over hard times. But, as ever, there were the professionals.

Professional Beggars

Professional beggars or those who had taken the *Salamon* - the beggars' sacred oath - were as specialised as any other profession.

Cadge Cloak; Maunder; Mumper	General term for a beggar
Abram Cove; Abram Man; Mad Tom; Tom of Bedlam	Near-naked beggar, pretending to madness
Autem Goggler	Pretended prophet
Blind Harpers	Beggar musicians pretending blindness, led by a child or dog
Clapperdogeon	A beggar born and bred
Domerar; Dromerar	Beggar who pretends to have had his tongue cut out, or to be born dumb and deaf
Flying Camp	Beggars plying as a group at funerals

Maund; Mump; Mung	To beg
Palliards	Those whose fathers were clapperdogeons, or beggars born, and who themselves follow the same trade
Rattling Mumpers	Beggars who ply coaches
Gaggers; Rum Gaggers	Cheats, who by sham stories of their sufferings, impose on the credulity of well meaning people
Fermerdy Beggars	All beggars who operate without sham sores or *Cleyms*
Rum Mawnd	Beggar who pretends to be a fool
Whip Jacks	Counterfeit mariners pretending to have been shipwrecked
Kinchin Coves; Kinchin Morts	Beggar children, often orphans
Sturdy Beggars	Beggars who demand rather than ask

Digression: Cleyms

Cleyms or *Clyms* are false sores created by beggars to create sympathy. The process of creating one is described as follows:

Cleyms are sores without Pain, raised on Beggars' Bodies, by their own Artifice and Cunning, (to move Charity) by bruising Crows-foot, Spearwort, and Salt together, and clapping them on the Place, which frets the Skin; then with a Linnen Rag, which sticks close to it, they tear off the Skin, and strew on it a little Powderd arsnick, which makes it look angrily or ill-favouredly, as if it were a real Sore.

Try this if you will but perhaps it would be better to leave off the powdered arsenic.

The *Cleyms* could be used in various ways:

Footman's Mawnd	An artificial sore made with unslaked lime, soap, and the rust of old iron, on the back of a beggar's hand, as if hurt by the bite or kick of a horse
Mason's Mawnd	A sham sore above the elbow, to counterfeit a broken arm by a fall from a scaffold
Soldier's Mawnd	A counterfeit wound, which a pretended soldier claims to have received at some famous siege or battle

CHAPTER FIFTEEN

Rogues on the Road

Everywhere you go there are Rogues in the city streets and on the highways. Those on the streets will likely pick your pocket. Those on the highway are more likely to demand money with menace.

Pickpockets

Being a pickpocket, once you have mastered the art, is one of the best of the dishonest professions.

You do not have to sneak around dark and dangerous streets at night, there is little or no violence involved, and London has more than a million pockets just begging to be picked.

Moreover, people tend to keep money in their pockets, thereby allowing you to bypass the *Lock* or *Fence* and keep it all for yourself.

If you are going to be a rogue, being a *Buz Cove* (pickpocket) is a good choice.

Digression: The Gentle Art of Picking Pockets

The earliest manifestation of the pickpocket is the *Bung Nipper* who would cut purses off the belt or girdle. By the Georgian period fashions had changed and purses and pocketbooks were carried in pockets. The criminal classes were forced to adapt and the art of *Forking* developed.

Forking is a technique whereby the fingers are held straight and stiff. The hand is thrust rapidly into the pocket and the fingers curl around anything they can find and withdraw. It requires practice but with suitable expertise it can be very effective.

Picking pockets becomes even easier if the victim is distracted. Thus, many *Divers* work with a *Bulk* or *Shoulder Sham*. This gentleman bumps into the victim or jostles them against a wall and the more dextrous partner moves in.

This technique still has one problem. If the victim suspects something and manages to take hold of the pickpocket, he is caught red-handed with the goods on his person. To deal with this problem the *Adam Tiler* is utilised.

As soon as the *Diver* or *File* has lifted the goods he passes them quickly to the *Adam Tiler* who disappears into the crowd. If the pickpocket is apprehended he can show he has no stolen goods. Meanwhile his partner is long gone - *Bought a Brush* in thieves' parlance.

Thus, while some pickpockets worked independently, a combination of *Bulk and File*, *Diver* and *Adam Tiler* or in the complete set of *Bulk*, *File* and *Adam Tiler* worked particularly well.

Adam Tiler	Confederate of a pickpocket who spirits away the stolen goods
Buz Cove; Buzman; Diver; Cly Faker; File; Knuckler	Pickpocket
Bulk; Shoulder Sham	Confederate of a pickpocket who bumps or jostles the victim
Autem Divers	Pickpockets who work church congregations
Dummy Hunters; Reader Merchants	Pickpockets who specialise in stealing pocketbooks
Snatch Cly	Pickpocket who steals from women
Creeme	Slip or slide anything into the hands of another
Draw	Take anything from a pocket
Grabble	Seize

Do not trust to your pockets to keep your possessions safe (this is good advice even now).

Highwaymen and Footpads

The movements of people and goods provide excellent opportunities for crime.

A mounted highwayman does not require much skill (apart from being able to ride a horse). He can overtake a carriage, stick a pistol through the window and demand money.

For a footpad things are a little trickier. There is no point in trying to bail up a man on a horse if he is just going to ride over the top of you. The trick is surprise and a clever footpad also works with a confederate. They hide behind a bank next to the road and then run out as a rider approaches. One grabs the bridle of the startled horse while the other deploys the secret weapon - a long pole with an iron hook on the end - to pull the rider to the ground. In this position he can be robbed and/or murdered according to the whim of the attackers.

Collector; High Pad; High Toby Gloak; Knight of the Road; Land Pirate; Rank Rider; Rum Padder; Scamp; Snaffler; Toby Gill; Toby Man	Mounted highwayman
Foot Pad; Low Pad	Highway robbers who work on foot
Bully Ruffians	Particularly vicious high-waymen or footpads

Royal Scamps	Highwaymen who never rob any but rich persons, and that without ill treating them
Colt	An innkeeper who lends horses to highwaymen
Banditti	General term for highway robbers, mounted or unmounted
Provender	He from whom any money is taken on the highway

Digression: Highwaymen

Being a highwayman was a bit of a hit-and-miss affair. You could get lucky and hold up an undefended coach full of rich people. Or you could be unlucky, get caught and be hanged shortly thereafter.

A strong contender for the least successful career on the highway is one John Smith. Executed in 1704 he is slightly outside our period but still useful as a Terrible Warning.

Taking to the road, he robbed ten coaches in three days, which at least showed commitment to his new profession.

However, all this hard work netted him only £20 - a nice sum of money but hardly worth risking your neck for.

Still not discouraged, he robbed the coach of a Mr Thomas Woodcock, netting four guineas, but he was spotted by a passing gentleman who pursued him and eventually caught him in a nearby wood.

Justice was swift and fourteen days later Smith was dead - dangling by his neck on the Tyburn gallows.

Somewhat more successful was John Rann, known as 'Sixteen-String Jack' for his habit of wearing breeches with eight strings at each knee. For a while he evaded the law. In 1774 he spent a lot of time in the dock at the Old Bailey:

April: For robbing Mr William Somers on the highway. Acquitted.

April: For robbing Mr Langford on the highway. Acquitted.

July: For robbing John Devall, Esq. of his watch and chain on Hounslow Heath. Acquitted.

July: For a burglary in Bow Street. Complaint dismissed.

September: Arrested for debt and incarcerated in Marshalsea prison. Bailed out by friends.

October: For robbing Dr. William Bell, chaplain to the Princess Amelia.

Alas, it was here that things went astray. Rann was so certain that he would be acquitted that he had ordered a supper afterwards to be enjoyed with his friends.

The jury thought otherwise and it was with shock that Rann heard the death sentence - *Cramp Words* as his companions would have called it - being handed down from the bench.

He showed little contrition and continued to enjoy life in his cell as much as possible including a particularly famous party involving seven women of uncertain reputation.

On the 30th November he was pushed off the cart at Tyburn and duly strangled to death.

Far more successful was the most famous highwayman of them all: Richard Turpin, more commonly known as Dick.

For most of the 1730s he pursued a life of crime which included not only the highway robbery for which he was best known but also cattle stealing, smuggling, deer poaching, house-breaking, demanding money with menaces, horse stealing and murder.

Between 1735 and 1737 he worked with a highwayman named King. This extremely successful and profitable partnership came to an unfortunate end when Turpin accidentally shot his companion.

Eventually, with a reward of £200 on his head, he found the south of England too hot for him and headed for Lincolnshire where he lived by horse-stealing for a while.

Finally his luck ran out and he was arrested although not recognised under the name of John Palmer.

However, Turpin wrote to his brother in Essex about his plight. His brother was too mean to pay sixpence to receive it (postal charges at this time being paid by the receiver, not the sender) so it was returned to the post office. It came to the attention of a magistrate who opened it and Turpin's real identity was discovered.

In a final act of drama, after his execution at York and burial in St George's churchyard, the body was dug up in the night.

The people of York, who had received Turpin with affection, tracked it down to the house of a surgeon and stole it back.

To discourage any further attempts at body-snatching they filled the coffin with quicklime and a rapidly dissolving Turpin was finally at rest.

Crimes on the Road

As a quick reminder, the following lays will be found in the streets and highways.

Drag Lay	Waiting in the streets to rob carts or wagons
Peter Lay; Flicking the Peter	Cutting portmanteaus and cloak bags from behind coaches
Prad Lay	Cutting bags from behind horses

Forms of Transport

It is worth reviewing the terms for different forms of transport available to be robbed. Strictly, most of these are slang words rather thieves' cant but you will hear them used.

Drag; Tumbler	Cart
Fly; Vardo	Wagon
Lock-up Chovey	Covered cart secured by door, lock and key
Leathern Convenience; Rattler	Coach
Rumble Tumble	Stage coach
Jack	Post chaise
Rotan	General term for a coach, wagon or cart
Unicorn	Coach drawn by three horses
Yarmouth Coach	A very slow cart, drawn by a single horse
Croppin	The tail of a vehicle

Horses

Although engineers such as William Murdoch were building prototype steam transport vehicles in the late 18th century and Richard Trevithick and George Stephenson developed them in the early 19th, public railways did not really get going until the Victorian period.

For the Georgians, the horse was the primary means of moving people and items on land.

Grogham; Keffal; Prad; Prancer; Tit	Horse
Galloper	A blood horse or hunter
Jacked; Piper; Queer Prancer; Rip; Roarer; Touched in the Wind	Broken-winded or worn-out horse
Kingswood Lion; Spanish Trumpeter; King of Spain's Trumpeter	Ass
Bishop	Concealing the age of a horse by burning a mark into a horse's tooth, after it has been lost through age
Bonesetter	A hard-trotting horse
Feague	To feague a horse; to put ginger up a horse's fundament, and formerly, as it is said, a live eel, to make him lively and carry his tail well
Gibbe	A horse that shrinks from the collar and will not draw
Grogged	Foundered (horse)
Gob; Gob String; Nab Girder; Nob Girder	Bridle

A *Scarlet Horse* is a hired or hack horse - a dreadful pun on hired = high red = scarlet.

Related Terms

Some transport-related terms are:

Feather Bed Lane; Jumble Gut Lane	Any bad or rough road
Jehu	A reckless driver
Rum Pad	The highway
Peter; Pogue; Roger	Portmanteau or cloak bag
Deuseaville	The country
Cracksmans; Ruffmans	Hedges or woods
Jague	Ditch

CHAPTER SIXTEEN

Rogues
in the House

Digression: Luxury for the Masses

The industrial revolution saw items previously considered luxuries now widely available to a burgeoning population. Mercantile endeavours brought wealth and spread it out to a much larger number of people - people who had disposable income rather than land and preferred it that way.

Kent's London Business Directory of 1740 lists 18 goldsmiths, 2 potters, 1 upholsterer, 16 hosiers, 2 glovers, 2 glassworkers and no perfumers or musical instrument makers. By 1794 the numbers have risen to 168 goldsmiths, 21 potters, 119 upholsterers, 230 hosiers, 39 glovers, 106 glassworkers, 53 perfumers and 23 makers of musical instruments. The rise in demand was enormous.

Housebreaking has always been one of the dishonourable professions but, with the greater abundance of small portable items of value, it now became a highly profitable business. Your friendly neighbourhood *Fence* or *Lock* was always ready to take your goods. Entire boatloads of stolen items made their way across the English Channel for ease of disposal.

Housebreakers

Housebreakers have their own special vocabulary. We have already encountered some of these terms in our section on *Rigs* and *Lays* but it is worth revising them. If you have left a door or window open, or even if you haven't, you may encounter some of them directly.

Housebreakers watch out for the *Gnarler* - a small dog that wakes everyone up with his barking when you try to break in. Dogs may also be referred to as *Buffs*, *Buffers*, *Bughers* or *Jugelows*. On the other hand the experienced *Mill Ken* ignores *Malkins* or *Tibbies* (cats) which, recognising him as being unlikely to be a source of food, equally ignore him.

Cracksman; Ken Miller; Ken Cracker; Mill Ken	General term for house-breaker
Budge; Sneaking Budge; Sneak	Thief who sneaks into houses where the door is unlocked
Darkmans Budge	Thief who sneaks into a house in the evening to let in confederates later at night

Snudge	Thief who hides under a bed, waiting for a chance to rob the house
Draw Latch	Thief who robs houses where the doors are only fastened with a latch
Glazier; Jumper	Thief who breaks in through windows
Kate; Dubber; Gilt	Lock picker

Crimes around the House

Dining Room Post	A mode of stealing in houses that let lodgings, by rogues pretending to be postmen, who send up sham letters to the lodgers, and, whilst waiting in the entry for the postage, go into the first room they see open, and rob it
Go upon the Hoist	To get into windows accidentally left open: this is done by the assistance of a confederate, called the *Hoist*, who leans his head against the wall, making his back a kind of step or ascent

Area Sneak; Area Slum	The practice of slipping unperceived down the areas of private houses, and robbing the lower apartments of plate or other articles.
Crack Lay	House-breaking
Dub Lay; Going upon the Dub	Robbing houses by picking locks
Mill Lay	Robbing houses by breaking in the doors
Shutter Racket	The practice of robbing houses, or shops, by boring a hole in the window shutter, and taking out a pane of glass

Building

Crib	House
Lumber; Slum	Room
Dancers	Stairs
Glaze	Window
Jump	Ground floor window
Back Jump	Back window
Back Slum	Back door
Jigger	Door
Moss	Lead, because both are found on top of buildings
Wicket	Casement or small door
Sky Parlour	The garret, or upper storey
Dunegan; Spice Islands	Privy

In the Bedroom

No one is going to steal *Oliver's Skull* but a *Rum Peeper* can always be fenced for a few shillings and some people will take the *Slate* from your *Libbege* without even thinking.

Dab; Libbege; Lig	Bed
Slat; Slate	Sheet
Jockum Gage; Jordan; Looking Glass; Member Mug; Oliver's Skull; Remedy Critch; Tea Voider	Chamberpot
Peeper; Shiner	Looking glass
Queer Peeper	Old or ordinary looking-glass
Rum Peeper	Silver looking-glass

Small Valuables and Tableware

Especially prized are small, valuable items that are easily transported, particularly for the *Area Sneak* who sneaks in and out of houses during *Lightmans* (daytime) and may have to *Pike* rapidly at any time.

Baubles; Moveables; Trinkets	Any small gold or silver objects
Lodge; Tatler; Thimble; Warming Pan	Watch
Sneezer; Sneezing Cofer	Snuffbox
Onion	Seal
Glimstick	Candlestick

Most tableware can also be slipped into a coat pocket.

Chop-Stick	Fork
Globe	Pewter
Jorum	Jug
Sneaker	Small bowl
Witcher Bubber	Silver bowl
Wedge	Silverware
Feeder	Spoon
Slop Feeder	Teaspoon
Os Chives	Bone-handled knives

Miscellaneous things around the House

Most of the following are not actually worth stealing but you may encounter the terms.

Chive; Chiff; Chury	Knife, saw or file
Glimmer	Fire
Jacob	Ladder
Glimfenders	Andirons
Lullies	Wet linen
Mill	Chisel
Muffling Cheat	Napkin
Princod	Pincushion
Smut	Copper boiler or furnace
Snipes	Scissors
Steel Bar	Needle
Sticks	Household furniture
Yokuff	Chest or large box

CHAPTER SEVENTEEN

Rogues all Around

Rogues are everywhere and pretty much anything that isn't nailed down is up for grabs. Your animals are certainly not safe. If you lose a dog you should advertise a reward as soon as possible. If a *Dog Buffer* gets hold of your pet its days are numbered.

Animal Specialists

Buff Knapper	Dog stealer
Buffer	One who kills horses and dogs for their skins
Dog Buffer	Dog stealer, who kills dogs not advertised for, sells their skins, and feeds them to the remaining dogs
Dunaker	Stealer of cows and calves
Napper; Napper of Naps	Sheep stealer
Prad Borrower; Prig Napper; Prigger of Prancers	Horse stealer
Prigger of Cacklers	Poultry stealer

More Rogues

Rogues are ingenious people and every little niche of dishonesty is filled. There are thieves who will steal the lead off your roof; thieves who will cheat the lotteries and even thieves who will pretend to sell you stolen goods! If you leave something valuable on a high window ledge a man with a hook on a long stick (an *Angler* or *Hooker*) will pilfer it. If it has value, a specialist exists to steal it.

Amusers	Rogues who carry snuff or dust in their pockets to throw into the eyes of the person they intended to rob
Anglers; Hookers	Pilferers, or petty thieves, who, with a stick having a hook at the end, steal goods out of shop-windows, grates, etc.
Ark Ruffians	Rogues who, in conjunction with watermen, rob, and sometimes murder, on the water, by picking a quarrel with the passengers in a boat, boarding it, plundering, stripping, and throwing them overboard

Badgers	A crew of desperate villains who rob near rivers, into which they throw the bodies of those they murder
Blue Pigeons	Thieves who steal lead off houses and churches
Clank Napper; Rum Bubber	Stealer of silver tankards from inns
Figger	A little boy put in at a window to hand out goods to the *Diver*
Fire Priggers	Villains who rob at fires under pretence of assisting in removing the goods
Lumpers	Thieves who lurk about wharfs to pilfer goods from ships, lighters, etc.
Natty Lads	Young thieves or pickpockets
Owlers	Those who smuggle wool over to France
Pigeons	Sharpers who get the results of a lottery then ride as fast as possible to a distant lottery office where they can place bets before the real news arrives

| Sham Leggers | Cheats who pretend to sell smuggled goods, but in reality only deal in old or damaged goods |
| Spruce Prigs | Well-dressed thieves who insert themselves into various festivities in order to steal from guests |

Digression: Spruce Prigs

Spruce Prigs were professional gate-crashers. Personable young men, well dressed and well mannered, they had little difficulty inserting themselves into the large social events where no one person knew everyone present. They would even arrive in hired carriages with their own servants (also thieves) for greater verisimilitude. These events offered rich pickings for a skilled thief.

In the 1720s, crime lord Jonathan Wild ran a nice system whereby his *Spruce Prigs* would steal all sorts of valuable trinkets at parties. At the same time, he ran a 'lost property office' whereby he would (for a suitable reward) manage to 'recover' said trinkets. Back with their original owners, the items were available to be stolen again. And so forth.

An example of just how convincing these young men could be is the tale of how a group of them convinced a society of bellringers that they too were devotees of the art and wagered £500 (an enormous sum of money) that they were better. When they met the following day at a country church, the real bellringers stripped off their hats and coats and climbed the belltower to show just how good they were. Wild's men promptly took said hats and coats, the wager money, the horses and the food that everyone had brought for lunch and decamped for a celebratory picnic elsewhere.

Even the royal court was not immune. One thief claimed that he was about to pick the pocket of King George I when, unfortunately, some woman pushed in before him so he picked her pocket instead. This sounds rather like the fishing story about 'the one that got away' but the fact that it was considered even plausible suggests an element of truth.

More Crimes

Christening	Erasing the name of the true maker from a stolen watch, and engraving a fictitious one in its place
Dead Men	A cant word among journeymen bakers, for loaves falsely charged to their master's customers
Fly a Blue Pigeon	Steal lead off houses or churches
Knuckle a Wipe	Steal a handkerchief

| Ring the Changes | Swap good shillings received as change for bad ones then insist that good ones be provided |
| Snap the Glaze; Star the Glaze | Break and rob a jeweller's show glass or a shop window |

Peachers and Whiddlers

Human beings being what they are, there is little honour among thieves. Apprehended gang members, given a choice between betraying their fellows and hanging, would seldom *Stand Buff*. Most decided that if someone had to hang it would be better if it were someone else.

Cackle	Give away secrets
Gnarl; Nose; Split	Betray
Blow the Gab	To confess, or impeach a confederate
Leaky; Long Tongued	Apt to blab
Lickspittle	A parasite, or talebearer
Queer Rooster	An informer
Slippery Chap	One on whom there can be no dependence, a shuffling fellow
Squeak; Turn Stag; Whiddle	To tell or discover
Turn Cat in Pan	To change sides or parties

CHAPTER EIGHTEEN

Violence

Violence was a fact of life in Georgian London. Dangerous gangs roamed the streets at night.

Crime was rife and weapons widely available. The police force was rudimentary or non-existent. There was no street lighting. If you needed to get about on a moonless night you hired a *Glimjack* - a boy who made a living by carrying a torch. On the whole you were better off staying inside once the sun had gone down.

Weapons

With the violence on the streets, particularly at night and in the rogue-infested areas you are visiting, carrying a weapon is recommended. Swords are by and large worn by gentlemen but you can get away with it in less respectable company.

The wearing of swords dies off as a fashion towards the end of the 18th century with swords primarily being used for duelling.

Pistols are the weapons of choice for the lower orders - easily concealed and requiring only limited skill at short range.

London has plenty of good sword cutlers. Earlier in the century I would recommend William Loxham at 88 Cornhill Street. He also has a good line in hats.

Later on you may wish to try His Majesty's own sword cutler, Callum, who operates at 9 Charing Cross Road. Or you can try his next-door neighbour Knubley at number 7 who doubles as a gun-maker.

His Majesty (George III) also patronises two gun-smiths - Charles Grierson at 10 New Bond Street and H.W. Mortimer at 89 Fleet Street. Joseph Manton's famous establishment at 25 Davies Street is also an excellent choice. Shop around. London has no shortage of quality gunsmiths.

If you are buying a pistol make sure you spend enough money to get a good one.

Up until 1820, when the percussion cap was invented, pistols worked by a flint striking against steel, creating a spark that sets off the loose gunpowder in the pan. Cheap pistols are likely to fail - flash in the pan - and possibly explode.

As all pistols are single shot you want to have the best possible chance of your shot getting off. Carrying a second pistol is recommended in the rougher areas.

Barking Irons; Bulldogs; Dags; Pops; Snappers; Sticks	Pistols
Bilboa; Bill; Cheese Toaster; Degen; Poker; Toasting Iron; Tol; Toledo	Sword
Queer Degen; Queer Tol	Ordinary sword with an iron or brass hilt
Rum Degen; Rum Tol	Silver hilted or inlaid sword
Chive; Chiv; Chury	Knife
Fivepenny; Sir Sydney	Clasp knife
Toothpick; Oaken Towel	Stick or cudgel
Jordain	Staff

Note the shortened forms *Bill* for Bilboa and *Tol* for Toledo, places where swords are manufactured.

Digression: Prize-fighting

In Georgian boxing circles John Sholto Douglas, the ninth Marquis of Queensberry, was not even a cloud on the horizon. His eponymous rules did not come into effect until 1867 (and were not, incidentally, written by him but by one Arthur Graham Chambers).

In the early years there were few rules and all knuckles were bare. The first recognised boxing champion, James Figg, did not receive this accolade until 1719 but he earned it - all sorts of what we would call foul play, including eye gouging, choking and kicking fallen opponents, were accepted and encouraged.

Things were regularised somewhat in 1734 when Jack Broughton formed the first boxing code. It was still pretty brutal by modern standards but at least eye-gouging and hitting fallen opponents were outlawed. Wrestling and rough fighting were still allowed and falling heavily on an opponent wrestled to the ground was deemed reasonable. There were no formal rounds - a round ended when one fighter's knee touched the ground or he was knocked down. Fights ended when one fighter gave in and they could go on for hours. *Broughtonian* remained an informal term for a fighter for the rest of the Georgian period.

Fatalities were not unknown. In 1812 one Edward Turner was convicted of manslaughter when his opponent, a man named Curtis, died following a bout. Witnesses swore that Curtis was repeatedly urged to give in but he shook off his seconds and continued fighting. Even Turner tried to convince him to stop but eventually Curtis was knocked out and never recovered consciousness. The judge and jury were sympathetic and Turner escaped with two months in Newgate Prison.

If you are an aficionado of the sport you should try and get to the fight in 1791 when Daniel Mendoza won the British Championship. Mendoza was the first really 'scientific' boxer, introducing techniques of defence, sidestepping and effective use of the straight left rather than relying on brute strength. You should also make a visit to the *Castle Tavern* in Holborn, the spiritual home of pugilists during the later Georgian period.

Bottom; Glutton	A boxer with good bottom is one who can endure a lot of punishment
Click in the Muns	Blow to the face
Chop	A kick or blow
Darken the Daylights; Queer the Ogles	Bruise a man around the eyes so he can't see
Hunch	Jostle or thrust
Muzzler	A violent blow on the mouth
Topper	Blow to the head
Twit	Blow to the teeth
Floor; Lay Trigging; Settle	Knock down
Dart	A straight-armed blow
Cock Hoist	A cross buttock throw
Flying Horse	A wrestling move to throw an opponent over your head
Fight a Crib	Make a sham fight
Fight at the Leg	Take unfair advantage
Vinegar	A man with a whip in his hand, and a hat held before his eye, whose task is to keep the ring clear

Violence-Related Terms

There are a large number of terms for being beaten. Consider why this is so before starting a fight in a *Flash Ken*.

Banged; Based; Basted; Chafed; Clawed Off; Dressed; Drubbed; Dumb Founded; Fagged; Fanned; Fibbed; Hooped; Laced; Lambasted; Poked; Pounded; Pummelled; Ribroasted; Sowred; Swaddled; Swinged; Tawed; Tuned	Beaten
Bell Swagger	A noisy bullying fellow
Bellyfull	A hearty beating, sufficient to make a man yield or give out
Cane upon Abel	A stick laid across a man's shoulders
Crack	Break
Culp; Nope; Pole; Stoter	A kick or blow
Cunny-Thumbed	To double one's fist with the thumb inwards, like a woman
Ding Boy	A rogue, a hector, a bully, or sharper
Figdean	Kill
Flip	Shoot

Mill	Do violence, from a beating to murder depending on context
Anoint with Oil of Gladness	Administer a beating
Smash	To break; also to kick down stairs
Snite	Wipe, or slap
Hack and Hue	Cut in pieces
At Daggers Drawing	Ready to fight

Digression: Young Bucks and Other Criminals

In the two-tier society that was Georgian London, there were groups of young men with too much money and too little gainful employment. They would roam the streets in search of entertainment and not care very much who got hurt.

Some of their activities counted as little more than common assault. *Boxing the Watch* was a favourite sport wherein a hapless watchman was pushed into his small wooden shelter, the opening nailed up and the shelter rolled down the street. All good fun unless you happened to be the one in the box in which case broken bones were a likely outcome.

A nastier trick was to set fire to a building late at night then laugh at everyone fleeing in their nightgowns. Quite often no-one would be burnt to death.

These essays into arson were roundly condemned but the perpetrators were usually men of influence, or at least the sons of such men, and as such were pretty much immune from prosecution.

The earlier years of the 18th century saw a number of gangs who made the London streets even more dangerous than normal.

The most famous were the Mohocks who named themselves after the Native American tribe. Lacking the courage and ferocity of those warriors, they made up for it by attacking those weaker than themselves.

One of their favourite pastimes was *Sweating*, which involved surrounding their victim in a circle.

The man behind the victim would prick him in the buttocks with a sword.

When he swung round to confront his attacker, the man behind would do the same.

They would spin their unfortunate target around until they tired of the whole exercise.

Worse practices involved disfigurement of the face with a knife or even cutting off ears as souvenirs.

A similar gang went by the name of Scourers who, according to their contemporaries, 'amuse themselves with breaking windows, beating the watch, and assaulting every person they meet'.

If you do go out at night, stay with the crowds or travel with well-armed companions.

Take this advice seriously - Georgian London at night is a very scary place.

Blood	A riotous disorderly fellow
Buck of the First Head	One who in debauchery surpasses the rest of his companions; a blood or choice spirit
Caterwauling	Going out in the night in search of intrigues, like a cat in the gutters
Hell Hound	A wicked abandoned fellow
Hunting the Squirrel	An amusement practiced by postboys and stagecoachmen, which consists in following a one-horse chaise, and driving it before them, passing close to it, so as to brush the wheel, and by other means terrifying any woman or person that may be in it
Wild Oats	He has sowed his wild oats; he is staid, or sober, having left off his wild tricks
Scapegrace	A wild, dissolute fellow
Spree	A frolic, drinking bout or party of pleasure

Digression: Duelling

Duelling is not something you are likely to encounter in the Georgian underworld. Not only is it traditionally the preserve of gentlemen but also no self-respecting rogue is going to stand up and let someone *Flip him with Barking Irons* or *Pink* him with a *Cheese Toaster*. Particularly if a surreptitious *Crack on the Costard* can lay his opponent unconscious.

If someone does challenge you to a duel, they have obviously mistaken you for someone important. Tell them you are flattered by their condescension but consider yourself unworthy of the honour. If they persist you will be taken for a coward if you refuse which may or may not worry you. You might consider accepting but not turning up, which will at least let you picture your opponent freezing in a cold field at dawn although the accusations of cowardice will persist.

Really, you should avoid duelling. It is illegal and, more to the point, people die in the process and you could either end up on a manslaughter charge or dead. If you absolutely must fight, consider wearing kevlar under your jacket.

Crashed; Hushed	Killed
Pink	Draw blood in a duel
Flip	Shoot
Tilt	Fight with a sword

CHAPTER NINETEEN

Judicial Punishment

While you could, in theory, be hanged for stealing a shilling it was not likely for so small an amount and there were a number of other punishments available.

Typically, the severity of the punishment was left to the discretion of the executioner, resulting in a nice little supplement to his income.

If you could *Grease his Fist* with a suitable *Dawb* or *Sop* (bribe) the punishment could become a lot easier to bear.

Branding

For a first offence, a thief might be branded or *Burned in the Hand*, typically with the letter 'M' for Malefactor. An apprehended felon who was discovered to have the brand mark could expect no further mercy.

Like so many things in this period, punishments might be mitigated by the application of money in the proper places. For a consideration, the officer of the court responsible for branding could be prevailed upon to use an iron less hot and perhaps not press so hard.

Badged; Charactered; Glimmed; Pawned	Burned in the hand
Juggler's Box	The branding equipment

Pillory

The medieval pillory remained in use throughout the Georgian period. Typically the sentence was for a number of uncomfortable hours, but the experience could vary drastically.

You could be sentenced to a whipping at the same time but the real issue was the mood of the crowd. Generally speaking you could expect to be pelted with rotten fruit, mud and excrement, and be filthy and stinking when released. If the mood of the crowd turned ugly you might receive hard objects as well with the potential for serious injury. *Beggars' Bullets* are stones.

Or you could be lucky. In 1703 Daniel Defoe published *The Shortest Way with Dissenters* - a satirical pamphlet suggesting that all Dissenters should be exterminated. He managed to offend the Established Church and the Dissenters both and was arrested and charged with seditious libel.

He was fined, sentenced to imprisonment and to a session in the pillory. The story goes that, such was his popularity, he was pelted with flowers rather than the more usual harmful or unhygienic objects.

Harmans; Norway Neckcloth; Nutcrackers; Penance Board; Picture Frame; Stoop; Wooden Ruff	Pillory
Babe in the Wood; Overseer; Stoop Napper; Surveyor of the Pavement	A criminal in the pillory
Stooping Match	Two or more people pilloried together

Imprisonment

Long term imprisonment was not a common punishment in Georgian England. Typically you would be either transported or hanged for any offence regarded as serious (which could be the theft of quite a small amount of money). A sentence of imprisonment was not likely to last more than a few months.

Digression: the Prisons of London

The prisons of Georgian London provide a classic example of the effects of unbridled private enterprise. Prisons were run for profit and in fact were so profitable that wardenships changed hands for thousands of pounds. There was no oversight of conditions and no checks on depredations.

Prisoners had to pay entry and (if they were lucky) exit fees. There were fees for accommodation, fees for food and drink, fees to have chains or manacles removed, and fees for anything else the warders might like to claim. Prisoners who could afford these services were known as *Milch-Kine* (milk cows).

Prisoners without means were lodged in over-crowded lice-ridden chambers from which death by disease or starvation was the most likely method of egress. The Fleet prison even had a special grille built into the Farringdon Street wall so that inmates without means could beg passers-by for money to buy food.

You could be imprisoned for failure to pay your debts (bankruptcy did not become an option until 1869). By a strange logic, you would remain in prison until the debts were paid but, while in prison, *you had no method of earning money*. Effectively you were there until some friend or relative paid your debts, or your creditors agreed to settle or forgive the debt, or for life. Sometimes, even payment of your debt was not enough. The warders could continue to hold you there until you had paid your 'chamber rent' - the charge for using your cell.

Of course, if you had money the prison experience was much improved. Newgate had a Master Felon's Area - a special area available for rent where your cell would be unlocked (although you could only get into a passageway). You could arrange (for a fee) to have servants and comfortable furniture brought in and (for another fee) good quality food and drink. In the Fleet Prison you didn't even have to live inside if you compensated the Keeper appropriately. You could live in an area called the 'Liberty of the Fleet', a defined area outside the prison.

Newgate Prison

Newgate was the main London prison in the Georgian period and the most famous of them all. The roll-call of its inmates includes Daniel Defoe (writer), Ben Johnson (playwright), Captain William Kidd (pirate), Titus Oates (anti-Catholic conspirator), William Penn (founder of Pennsylvania), Giacomo Casanova (libertine) and Jack Sheppard who escaped from it (twice) in 1724. It appears in many novels and plays including Charles Dickens' *Oliver Twist*, Daniel Defoe's *Moll Flanders* and John Gay's *The Beggar's Opera*.

There had been a prison on or near London's New Gate since the 12th century. The prison was burned down in the Great Fire of 1666 and rebuilt in 1672 by the executors of Lord Mayor Richard Whittington (he of the cat). One of the canting terms for Newgate prison is *The Whit*. An extension to the prison was begun in 1770, badly damaged in the Gordon Riots of 1780, and eventually finished in 1782. The prison was finally closed in 1902 and demolished in 1904. The Central Criminal Court now stands upon the site.

Newgate was where condemned criminals were held in dimly-lit cells called *Salt Boxes*.

Fleet Prison

Fleet Prison was located on the east side of the Fleet River (or Ditch as it was more appropriately known) and from which it took its name. In the Georgian period it was principally used to house debtors.

Its history is similar to that of Newgate - founded in the 12th century, destroyed in the Great Fire of 1666, rebuilt, destroyed again in the Gordon Riots of 1780, rebuilt in 1782 and finally closed down in 1844.

Until the Marriage Act of 1753, the Fleet Prison was the site of many hurried or clandestine marriages. Although churches had been obliged since 1695 to require either banns or a licence, the Fleet, being a prison not a church, was not covered by the Act. A whole industry grew up to support it in the Liberty of the Fleet area with taverns acting as venues and employing barkers to bring in custom. Disreputable clergymen and clerks were readily available for the formalities. The prison warders, of course, took their percentage.

After the 1753 Act, the industry collapsed and the bride and groom had to make the long trek to Gretna Green in Scotland where English rules did not apply.

Marshalsea Prison

Marshalsea, located south of the Thames in Southwark was, like the Fleet Prison, primarily for debtors although it was also used by the Admiralty to hold prisoners awaiting Court Martial.

Marshallsea was divided into two parts - the Master's Side and the Common Side. The Master's Side had about 50 rooms to rent at ten shillings a week, and had a bar, a chop house, a chandler's shop, a tailor, a barber and a coffee shop. The Common Side had 9 rooms containing 300 people and was a place of horror with the inmates crowded, filthy and starving, subject to beating and torture as their guardians saw fit. The Warden, William Acton, was tried for murdering one of the inmates in 1729 but he had little trouble in escaping the charge.

By the end of the century the prison had fallen into disrepair and was replaced in 1811 with conditions only slightly less cramped. It was finally closed in 1842.

Block House; Boarding School; Iron Doublet; Limbo; Nask; Naskin; Queer Ken; Quod; Rumbo; Sheriff's Hotel; Shop; Start; Steel; Stone Doublet; Stone Jug; Stone Tavern; Trib	Prison
City College; Newman's Hotel; Newman's Tea Gardens; The Whit	Newgate
Lud's Bulwark	Ludgate prison
Navy Office	Fleet prison
Canary Birds; Jail Birds	Prisoners
Salt Boxes	The condemned cells at Newgate

Angling for Farthings	Begging out of a prison window with a cap, or box, let down at the end of a long string
Lock up House; Spunging House	A public house kept by sheriff's officers, to which they convey the persons they have arrested
Campbell's Academy	The hulks or lighters, on board of which felons are condemned to hard labour (Mr. Campbell was the first director of them)

Steel is a shortening of Bastille.

Transportation

Marinated; Lumped the Lighter	Transported
Lag	Transportation for seven or more years
Winder; Bellowser	Transportation for life
Barrow Man; Lag	Convict under sentence of transportation
Old Lag	Person returned secretly from transportation
Lagging Dues	Transportation
Lag Ship	A ship for transportation; also a prison hulk
Cross the Herring Pond at the King's expense	To be transported

Returning from transportation before sentence expired was a hanging offence.

Whipping

Push the Cart and Horses Too; Take Air and Exercise; Shove the Tumbler	Whipped at the cart's tail
Jigger	Flogging post
Hued; Rumped; Tatted; Teazed	Flogged
Fly Flapped	Flogged in the stocks or at the cart's tail
Show your Shapes	To be stripped at the whipping-post
Strong man	To play the part of the strong man, i.e. to push the cart and horses too; to be whipped at the carts tail

As always, the degree of severity was left to the discretion of the executioner who, it was said, had a cat of nine tails for all budgets.

CHAPTER TWENTY

Death and Capital Punishment

Death, of course, comes to all of us sooner or later. But for the rogues of Georgian London it always had the chance of coming sooner.

Capital punishment was a serious risk and this is reflected in number of words and phrases for being hanged.

Many also had a fear of being *Ottomised* or dissected by the surgeons. There are a number of cases of friends and relatives snatching bodies from the gallows to prevent them ending up on the dissecting table in front of a class of medical students.

Rogues called *Resurrection Men* would fill this demand for corpses by robbing graves, and the surgeons asked no questions. At approximately 4 guineas per corpse, it wasn't a bad way to make a living.

Death

Backed; Croaked; Gone to Peg Trantums; Kicked the Bucket	Dead
Content	Past complaining i.e. a person murdered for resisting robbers
Earth Bath; Ground Sweat	A grave
Eternity Box; Scold's Cure; Wooden Habeas; Wooden Surcoat	Coffin
Cool Crepe	Shroud
Barrel Fever	Drinking yourself to death
Ottomised	Dissected
Dustman	Dead man
Put to bed with a mattock and tucked up with a spade	Dead and buried
Put to bed with a shovel	Buried

Hanging

Capital punishment in England was almost always by hanging, although peers and important gentlemen might be decapitated with an axe instead. Women who had committed treason (which included murdering their husbands) were burnt at the stake. The executioner would nearly always strangle the woman before the flames reached her but there is at least one horrific case where he failed to do so.

But hanging was the most common punishment although far more were sentenced to death than actually hanged.

Digression: Death by Hanging

For most of the Georgian period, hanging was not the (reasonably) fast and (allegedly) painless death that it later became. The *Triple Tree* at Tyburn (near where Marble Arch stands today) consisted of three massive horizontal beams arranged in a triangle. Cant terms such as the *Three Legged Mare* reflect its shape. A noose was tied over the beam and the prisoner stood on a cart or a ladder. When the ladder was taken away or the cart driven off the victim swung into the air and slowly strangled to death. Up to twenty-four simultaneous hangings could take place although this seldom happened.

Hanging day or *Paddington Fair* attracted large crowds and generated a lot of business for both pie-sellers and pickpockets. The prisoner was transported from Newgate Prison to Tyburn on a cart while sitting on his coffin and with a noose around his neck. It could take several hours to get there if the crowds were heavy. The condemned were allowed alcohol and the sensible ones were as drunk as possible when the fatal moment arrived.

To add insult to asphyxiation, you were charged for the privilege - 6s 8d. Those who could not afford it were buried in a pit under the gallows.

Tyburn continued to operate until 1783 when executions were moved to be outside Newgate Prison.

Failed Executions

In November 1740 William Duell was hanged for murder. After he had hung for the requisite time his body was taken to the Surgeons' Hall. He was laid out on a board for an anatomy class when he was seen to be moving and subsequently recovered his senses, although he had no memory of the hanging itself.

On Christmas Eve 1705 a man named John Smith was hanged at Tyburn but after he had hung for about 15 minutes a reprieve came through so he was cut down and, to the amazement of all, successfully revived. Smith did remember his execution and in the Newgate Calendar his experience is described as follows:

When he had perfectly recovered his senses he was asked what were his feelings at the time of execution; to which he repeatedly replied, in substance, as follows.

When he was turned off, he for some time was sensible of very great pain, occasioned by the weight of his body, and felt his spirits in a strange commotion, violently pressing upwards.

That having forced their way to his head, he as it were saw a great blaze, or glaring light, which seemed to go out at his eyes with a flash, and then he lost all sense of pain.

That after he was cut down, and began to come to himself, the blood and spirits, forcing themselves into their former channels, put him, by a sort of pricking or shooting, to such intolerable pain that he could have wished those hanged who had cut him down.

For the rest of his life he was known as Half-hanged Smith.

Technically you could be hanged again but it appears that this was seldom the case. Smith was pardoned and Duell's sentence was commuted to transportation.

There are other cases but seldom with so happy an outcome due to brain damage from lack of oxygen. One hesitates to think about the possibility of being *Put to Bed with a Shovel* (buried) or *Ottomised* without being completely dead.

Chates; Crap; Gregorian Tree; Morning Drop; Newman's Lift; Nubbing Cheat; Scragging Post; Sheriff's Picture Frame; Topping Cheat; Three Legged Mare; Three Legged Stool

The gallows

Dance at Beilby's Ball; Climb Three Trees with a Ladder; Crapped; Cry Cockles; Dance at the Sheriff's Ball; Dance the Paddington Frisk; Dance upon Nothing; Dangle; Frummagemmed; Jammed; Gone up the Ladder; Nubbed; Scragged; Stretched; Swung; Topped; Twisted Collar Day; Paddington Fair	Hanged

Execution day |
Piss when you can't Whistle; Ride a Horse foaled by an acorn	To be hanged
Kick the Clouds before the Hotel Door	To be hanged outside the prison
Wry Mouth and a pair of Pissen Breeches	Hanging
Hempen Widow	A woman whose husband has been hanged
Anodyne Necklace	Halter

A psalm sung at the gallows is called the *Dismal Ditty*.

One who deserves to be hanged but has thus far escaped this fate is called a *Scapegallows* or *Slipgibbet* and is one for whom the gallows are said to groan. A *Hang-Gallows Look* is a thievish appearance. A *Hang-in-Chains* is a vile, desperate fellow.

CHAPTER TWENTY-ONE

Women and Sex

Women

Women in the Georgian period were not seen as the equals of men. In canting terms they are nearly always referenced via sex - either marriage and childbearing, or prostitution or, for female rogues, their profession.

Article; Cooler; Dodsey; Flat Cock; Laced Mutton; Mollisher; Mot; Mort; Piece	General term for woman
Cambridge Fortune	Signifies a woman with only personal endowments
Giggler; Tib; Titter	A young woman
Gimcrack	A spruce wench
Gunpowder	An old woman
Jack Whore	A large masculine woman
Jade	A term of reproach to women
Su-Pouch	Hostess or landlady
Thornback	An old maid

Marriage

Smithfield Bargain	Marriage contracted solely on the score of interest, on one or both sides, where the fair sex are bought and sold like cattle in Smithfield
Live under the Cat's Foot	Hen-pecked
Hand Basket Portion	A woman whose husband receives frequent presents from her father, or family, is said to have a hand-basket portion
Apron-String Hold; Petticoat Hold	One who has an estate during his wife's life
Pin Money	An allowance settled on a married woman for her pocket expenses
Lawful Blanket	A wife
Bill of Sale; House to Let	A widow's weeds

Pregnancy

Broken Leg	A woman who has had a bastard is said to have broken a leg
Face-Making	Begetting children
Coming Wench	Pregnant woman
Poisoned	Big with child
Sprained her ankle	Pregnant

Sex

The Georgian period was no different to the modern one in terms of the amount of thought and energy expended on sex but venereal disease, in the absence of antibiotics, was far more prevalent.

As always, there were prostitutes. At a time when there were few options for unmarried women, prostitution was often seen as a superior choice to starvation. It was quite often a part-time profession - when times were hard the income could be enough to tide the family over the bad patch. At the lower end of the profession life expectancy was short, with syphilis being the great killer.

Sex was mostly unprotected. Condoms did exist but the process of vulcanising rubber was not discovered until 1839 so they were made of either animal intestines or (in the earlier period) linen soaked in vinegar. As such, their popularity was limited.

The injunction against young gentlewomen consorting with known rakes or philanderers was not just a question of morals. It also addressed the very real risk of contracting venereal disease from these convivial gentlemen.

Bube; Burnt; Crinkums; Covent Garden Gout; Drury Lane Ague; Flap Dragon; French Disease; French Gout; Frenchified; Peppered; Shot twixt Wind and Water; Spanish Gout; Sunburnt	Venereal disease
Dripper; Pissing Pins and Needles	Gonorrhoea
Dropping Member; Running Horse; Running Nag	Penis with gonorrhoea
Blue Boar; Shanker	Venereal wart
Scotch Fiddle; Scrubado; Welsh Fiddle	The itch
Fire Ship	A wench who has the venereal disease
Cannikin; Token	Plague or venereal disease
Laid up in Job's Dock	In treatment for venereal disease: Job's Ward, in St. Bartholomew's hospital was for venereal patients
Lock Hospital	A hospital for venereal patients

A *Blow with the French Faggot Stick* refers to the nose being lost or fallen in due to syphilis.

Lovers and Lechers

Goat; Hell-born Babe; Hell Hound; Man of the Town; Rake; Rakehell; Rakeshame; Town Bull	Lecher or lewd and debauched fellow
Corinthian	Frequenter of brothels
Duddering Rake	A buck of the first head, one extremely lewd
Dark Cully	A married man who keeps a mistress and creeps to her in the night for fear of discovery
Colt's Tooth	An old fellow who marries or keeps a young girl, is said to have a Colt's Tooth in his head
Mutton Monger	Man addicted to wenching; also a sheep stealer
Top Diver	Lover of women
Buck Fitch	A lecherous old fellow
Take a Slice	To intrigue, particularly with a married woman, because a slice off a cut loaf is not missed

Brothels

You are strongly advised not to visit the brothels (see above for warnings about venereal diseases). If you must do so, please *Fight in Armour* i.e. use condoms. They are

mostly made of sheep's intestines. The best place to pur-
chase them is from Mrs Phillips at the *Green Canister* in
Half-moon street in the Strand.

Molly Houses were places where men could have sex
with each other but were more a type of club than a
brothel. They were generally tolerated but, since the
Buggery Act of 1533, sodomy was a capital offense so in
the event of a raid a rapid retreat out the back entrance
was desirable.

Academy; Buttocking Shop; Cavaulting School; Civil Reception House; Corinth; Nanny House; Nugging House; Punch House; Pushing School; School of Venus; Seraglio; Smuggling Ken; Snoozing Ken; Vaulting School	Brothel
Fight in Armour	Use a condom

Madams and Pimps

Abbess; Aunt; Bawd; Buttock Broker; Mackerel; Madam Van; Mother; She-Napper	Madam
Beard Splitter; Bull; Cock Bawd; Gap Stopper; Stallion	Pimp or whoremaster
Pimp Whiskin	Top flight pimp

Prostitutes

Prostitutes in this context are nearly all women although there are a few words for men charmingly described as 'kept by a lady for secret services'.

I have attempted to divide the terms into Mistresses (who mostly serviced a single gentleman) and Prostitutes who had a variety of clients. The division is a fuzzy one and some terms overlap but it provides a rough guide.

Convenient; Left-handed Wife; Miss; Natural; Rum Blower	Mistress
Barber's Chair; Blowen; Bob-tail; Burick; Buttock; Cat; Covent Garden Nun; Crack; Drury Lane Vestal; Family of Love; Fen; Giggler; Laced Mutton; Light Frigate; Merry Arse Christian; Mab; Mob; Moll; Mott; One of my Cousins; Punk; Trull; Woman of the Town; Wagtail	Prostitute
Wasp	An infected prostitute (i.e. with a sting in the tail)
Drab; Quean	Low-class prostitute

Bat	Low-class prostitute - so called because she moves out in the dusk
Buttock and File	Prostitute who is also a pickpocket
Buttock and Twang; Down Buttock and Sham File	Prostitute who is specifically not a pickpocket
Case Vrow	Prostitute attached to a particular brothel
Fancy Man; Petticoat Pensioner; Stallion	A man kept by a lady for secret services
Bunter	A low dirty prostitute, half whore and half beggar
Covey	Collective noun for prostitutes

Socket Money is the fee for services rendered.

Sex

Basket Making; Blanket Hornpipe; Buttock Ball; Clicket; Dance the Goat's Jig; Dock; Hump; Jock; Lib; Moll Peatly's Gig; Occupy; Prig; Quiff; Relish; Rut; Screw; Strap; Stroke; Tiff; Shag; Strum; Swive; Touch up; Tup; Two handed put; Vault; Wap	Copulate

Blow off the Loose Corns	Occasional sex
Box the Jesuit; Toss Off	Masturbate
Back Door Usher; Back Gammon Player; Indorser; Madge Cull; Molly; Navigator of the Windward Passage	Those who indulge in sodomy
Blow off the Groundsils	Have sex on the floor or stairs
Buttered Bun	Lying with a woman who has just lain with another man
Chuck	To show a propensity for a man
Flogging Cully	An old lecher, who, to stimulate himself to venery, causes himself to be whipped with rods
Take a Flyer	To enjoy a woman with her clothes on, or without going to bed
Made a Duchess	Said of a woman having sex where one or both parties are wearing boots or shoes
Riding the Dragon; Riding Rantipole; The Dragon Upon St George	Sex with the woman on top
Keeping Cully	One that maintains a mistress

CHAPTER TWENTY-TWO

Returning Home

Congratulations! You have survived your foray into the Georgian underworld. You have managed to avoid being hanged, murdered, killed in a riot or dying of disease or starvation.

You are now a *Bowman Prig*, a *Dimber Damber* and can pass as a *Queer Cove* in the lowest company. You may have picked up some antisocial skills such a *Faking a Cly* or *Dubbing a Jigger*. Use these with discretion when you get home.

Finally, it is likely that you were never formally *Stalled to the Rogue* - inducted into roguish society - so I shall take it upon myself to perform the duties of the *Upright Man*:

I, The Author do stall thee, The Reader to the rogue; and from henceforth it shall be lawful for thee to cant for thy living in all places.

You now have the power. Use it wisely.

Academic Stuff

You don't need to read this to function in the Georgian underworld but for those interested in following further, here are some notes.

You should be aware that this book is of only limited academic utility. Here are a few of the problems and points of interest:

1. The Concept of Georgian England

Firstly, while I have treated the period as a single entity, the whole concept of 'Georgian England' is not a very useful one. About the only things that the years 1714 (when George I became King) and 1830 (when George IV breathed his last) have in common is that the backsides sitting on the throne of England all belonged to Hanoverian men named George.

Britain of 1714 was an agrarian economy where the majority of the population worked the land. London had a population of half a million (still huge by the standards of the day) and the first steam engine had yet to percolate through Trevithick's brain. Roads were appalling (the journey from London to Bath took 50 hours) and mobility was thus poor. The majority of the population died in the village or town where they were born.

With the Hanoverian succession, the ruling classes plunged their trotters firmly into the political trough and Robert Walpole built his magnificent residence at Houghton Hall on the strength of it. Corruption was rife, the laws draconian and the great landowners were solidly in the saddle of State.

Then came the Industrial Revolution and the world turned upside down.

Money is power and suddenly there were incredibly wealthy men who did not own vast country estates and had no desire to do so. Their power came from their manufactories and their trading vessels. Their power shook the comfortable foundations of rural England.

Turnpike roads were built along the major routes, facilitating the movement of people and goods. A turnpike gate, incidentally, is known as a *Flying Jigger* and the toll collector as the *Dub at a Knapping Jigger*. The aforementioned 50 hour trip to Bath shrank to a mere 16 hours. You could reach London from Edinburgh in 60 hours. In 1714 the advertised time was 256 hours.

There is simply no comparison between London in 1714 and London in 1830.

2. Canting Dictionaries and Source Material

The first stand-alone dictionary of canting terms (as opposed to glossaries in other works) is *A New Dictionary of the Terms ancient and modern of the Canting Crew*, written by the anonymous "B.E., Gent". and published in 1698.

Every slang and canting dictionary of the next 125 years is derived (if not outright plagiarised) from this work with new terms being added as the later authors thought appropriate.

Over the next forty years we have:

1719: *Thieves' New Canting Dictionary* in Captain Alexander Smith's *History of the Lives and Robberies of the Most Notorious Highwaymen.*

1725: *New Canting Dictionary* by an anonymous author.

1737: "*Collection of Canting Words*" in Bailey's Universal Etymological English Dictionary.

1750 et seq: the glossary in *Life of the self-styled gypsy king Bamfylde Moore Carew* is essentially B.E.'s work

A significant expansion of B.E.'s text was made in The *Classical dictionary of the Vulgar Tongue*, published by Captain Francis Grose in 1785.

The work was substantially expanded for a second edition in 1788 and a third in 1796. While it uses B.E.'s material as a base this is a new and original piece of lexicography and valuable as such.

In 1811 it was pirated by 'a member of the whip club' assisted by several others, one of whom went by the colourful name of 'Hell-Fire Dick'. It was known as the *Lexicon Balatronicum* and was effectively the fourth edition of *The Classical dictionary*.

According to an entry in the Lexicon, Hell-Fire Dick was

> *The Cambridge driver of the Telegraph. The favourite companion of the University fashionables, and the only tutor to whose precepts they attend.*

One has visions of young bloods in an alehouse hanging on his every word and scribbling down all his favourite aphorisms. Mr Dick's lexographical credentials are an imponderable.

While the speed at which language changed did not compare to the modern era of mass communication and the Internet, nevertheless it is disingenuous to assume, as I have done, that thieves' cant at the beginning of the period is the same as it is at the end.

The various dictionaries and glossaries provide us with a *terminus post quem* for each term. That is, once a word has appeared in print we know it existed from at least the date of that publication.

Unfortunately, this does not tell us when a word went out of use. The problem is seriously exacerbated by the ongoing plagiarisation of B.E.'s original text. The mere appearance of a word in the *Lexicon Balatronicum* that is also in B.E.'s work does not guarantee that it was still in use in 1811.

In this book (*mea culpa*) I have freely mixed terms from the different periods. Since the majority of our words come from the later period - Grose's work is considerably larger than B.E.'s and it too was expanded - it reflects the later Georgian period better than the early.

How much of this is actual thieves' cant is hard to say. Much of it clearly belongs to upper class student witticisms. I have removed the terms which are obviously classical puns but many remain.

Our best indication of whether a term is actually used by the criminal orders is whether it appears in glossaries like that of James Hardy Vaux (in 1819) which are not derived from B.E.. Vaux belonged to the genuine Georgian thieving classes and may be considered reasonably reliable.

Unfortunately, his glossary was produced to be read by the Governor of New South Wales and his ilk so references to sex and other unmentionable topics do not appear.

If you want a proper analysis you should consult a serious work such as Jonathan Green's *Dictionary of Slang*.

3. Thomas Harman and the Orders of Rogues

As always in this period (and not uncommonly today), authors often take earlier work without acknowledgement. The Orders of Rogues in Chapter 12 date back to 1566 in a book by Thomas Harman *A Caveat or Warning for Common Cursitors, vulgarly called Vagabonds*. Harman appears to have had genuine contact with beggars but did not see his categories as being fixed or all-inclusive as later writers assume. They were included in B.E.'s work and thus all the 18th century and later derivatives.

However accurate Harman's descriptions were in 1566, it is unlikely that they reflected the state of things two centuries later. I have included them in this book because they are interesting and fun and may still be of some relevance to the Georgian underworld.

More Information

The online *Proceedings of the Old Bailey* (*www.oldbaileyonline.org*) are an absolute treasure-trove of information with accounts of trials from 1674 through to 1913. Well worth a visit.

There are innumerable printed works about the Georgian period in general. Here is a small selection to get you going:

Anything by Roy Porter is worth reading. *English Society in the 18th Century* is a good place to start

Patrick Dillon has written a wonderful book about the gin craze entitled *The Much-lamented Death of Madam Geneva.*

Tim Hitchcock's *Down and Out in Eighteenth-Century London* is a good description of life at the bottom.

For the other end of the scale see Mancine Berg's *Luxury and Pleasure in Eighteenth-Century Britain.*

If you are planning another trip, you may also care to visit the author's website at *www.pascalbonenfant.com* where you will find a lot more information on the period.

Stephen Hart, March 2014

Read on for an excerpt from the author's historical urban fantasy, set in the years 1724-1725.

Available now at www.amazon.com.

THE UNFORTUNATE DEATHS OF JONATHAN WILD

BEING THE FIRST VOLUME OF
THE MEMOIRS OF PASCAL BONENFANT
TOGETHER WITH EXTRACTS FROM
THE DIARY OF ROSE VERNEY

Prologue

The storm came out of nowhere.

The First Mate looked in disbelief at the sky as the scattered clouds were drawn together as if by a giant hand. As they gathered, they turned black and lightning flashed. A giant swell began to build with waves towering up above the side of the ship. The ship heeled over as the swell and a sudden gale slammed into it. It had taken maybe one minute.

"All hands!" he yelled.

The crew were already moving. Alerted by the sudden swell they poured out onto the deck and climbed desperately up the rigging. They were a good, experienced crew and they knew that they must shorten sail and quickly.

The bosun's whistle sounded shrill above the now howling wind, piping out instructions to the men aloft. The ship rocked and men fought to keep their grip as they spread out across the yardarms.

The rain started, drenching everyone in seconds. Hailstones the size of a man's fist fell, tearing holes in the sails. One sailor was hit in the head and fell stunned into the sea.

The First Mate had no time to look. He was wrestling with the wheel, trying to keep the ship on a safe heading. The Captain appeared beside him and together they hauled desperately.

They were winning, the First Mate thought. The sails were shortening and already handling was becoming easier. They were the best crew he had ever worked with – he had never seen sails taken in so fast. He thought he might yet see his wife and children in Portsmouth once again.

Suddenly, the wheel spun in his hand and there was a loud crack, sounding like a cannon above the gale.

"Rudder's gone!" he shouted unnecessarily. Every man on board knew what the sound meant.

The ship started to turn slowly. We could still survive, he thought. The masts would probably go but if we could cut them loose the ship might bob around until the storm blew away. It couldn't be long. Already he thought he saw a patch of blue sky in the distance.

As he watched, the small speck of colour grew and he realised it wasn't sky at all but a patch of putrescent grey-blue. It wasn't growing, it was getting closer.

A slash of yellow appeared on the front of whatever it was and through the lashing rain he could see small, red dots on its surface. As it grew closer and closer he realised it was enormous, almost as big as the ship.

The details resolved themselves and the yellow slash became a huge mouth, lined with teeth, each the length of a man's arm and the thickness of his thighs. A greenish liquid dripped from bloated lips and hissed as the rain hit it.

The red dots became eyes, hundreds of them peering hungrily in all directions. The whole thing glowed in the dim light like poisonous toadstools in a forest of rotting wood.

The first mate screamed. All thoughts of duty, family and even of survival were lost in an overwhelming madness of terror.

A drop of green liquid from the creature's mouth fell on his arm and he felt an agonising pain as it burned through the rough cloth of his jacket. It barely had time to register before the massive jaws closed on him, crushing and swallowing him in an instant before turning to its next victim.

Men ran and leapt into the sea, screaming or praying according to their natures. Nothing made any difference. All were overwhelmed by the horror in the sky and devoured.

*   *   *

The lookout on a Newcastle coal ship, passing the spot a few hours later, saw what looked like the shattered remains of a large trading ship. The Captain ordered a boat across to look for survivors but there were none, not even any bodies. He said a brief prayer for the fate of its crew and then set sail again for land. Ships foundered all the time. Being a sailor was a dangerous trade.

Chapter 1

They hanged Jack Sheppard on 16th November 1724 and everyone except Jack enjoyed the day out. He was the darling of the London mob, famous for his impossible escapes from Newgate Prison. Tyburn Road was thronged with well-wishers – young women threw him flowers and men cheered him. Even the ghosts of former executions applauded although no one but me noticed.

At the triple tree itself he made a fine show, waving carelessly to the crowd as the rope was tied over the bar. Then they whipped up the horse and he swung off the cart into eternity.

It was good for business. Pie men and milkmaids cried their wares and sold them rapidly to the hungry and thirsty crowd. Flower sellers coined enough profit for several weeks. The hangman made a fortune selling the rope for sixpence an inch. And my friend Todd and I picked some rich pockets in the dense and raucous Tyburn crowd.

There was a riot afterwards with a fight over Jack's body but it broke up when they sent in the Marshall's men with bayonets. It was a good riot because Todd picked a pocketbook out of a prosperous pocket and it contained about twenty guineas in gold and silver, various documents and a banknote for one hundred and twenty pounds, nine shillings and fourpence. I remember the amount well for it represented a good year's thieving for us and we went and celebrated enthusiastically.

It was late by the time Todd and I climbed the three flights of dirty wooden stairs back to our room. We had been celebrating since the late afternoon and we were very drunk. Our new clothes were rumpled and stained with drink and dirt. The lace at the bottom of my coat was torn and Todd's stockings were laddered. It had truly been a wonderful debauch and we had enjoyed every minute.

Todd slipped on a stair where someone had spilt some oil and went crashing back to the landing. Drunk as he was, he landed sprawling and without damage and we both laughed uproariously. I went and helped him up and, leaning heavily on each other, we stumbled upward, still giggling at his mishap. No one came out of their room to complain of the noise. It was not the sort of neighbourhood where you did that.

There was a light under our door. We stopped giggling and looked at each other dubiously. Even drunk as we were we knew this was wrong – we had definitely not left a candle burning when we left and, in any case, it would have burned down after all those hours. I listened carefully and thought I heard a deep snuffling sound like some sort of large dog, although that was hardly likely. Who would take a dog up all those stairs?

In imitation of gentlemen we were both wearing short swords. Neither of us knew how to use them properly but they were sharp. With a single thought we both took them out. Todd managed to cut his left hand in the process and swore. We could, I suppose, have just walked away, but we were cocksure and valiant with drink. Todd lifted a foot and, managing not to fall over, kicked open the door.

Sitting in the room's single chair was a man, reading a book by the light of a pair of candles. There was nothing particularly alarming about him. He was slim, neatly but unobtrusively dressed and of average height. His sober coat of grey wool hung open to reveal a plain moleskin waistcoat and breeches. His wig was smaller than was fashionable then. There was a three-cornered hat sitting on our small table. As we made our violent entrance he looked up, unconcerned, and carefully placed a strip of leather between the pages to mark his place before he put the book down beside his hat.

Outraged, Todd stumbled drunkenly towards him, his sword pointing at the man's chest. "Get out!" he said violently. "Get out before I run you through!" His speech was slightly slurred but his intent was more than clear. I followed him in, waving my own sword vaguely. The neat man seemed unworried.

"Hook," he said softly.

Todd and I had a second to wonder what he meant, then the door slammed shut behind us with a crash. We jumped and turned and recoiled in horror. The candle-light flickered on a large, roughly dressed man and I very nearly pissed into my breeches. He was a dreadful sight.

At some point in his past he had lost the lower part of his left arm and had instead the wickedly curved hook that clearly explained the neat man's meaning and gave him his name. He stood awkwardly and at a slight angle suggesting injuries to his legs as well. But London is full of such sights. Far more horribly, you could see the great pox had its cold fingers tearing deep into his flesh.

His nose was a ghastly, rotting mess, oozing pus, and his breath came in a harsh bubbling noise – unforgettable and hideous. How I could have mistaken it for a dog, I had no idea. The smell of decay hung about him, of rotting flesh that is dying but not yet dead. The disease had deformed his face and twisted his lips into the parody of a grin, contrasting insanely with the near-dead eyes above. You could not imagine getting mercy from this monster. You could not even imagine him understanding any plea you might make. To our horror he started to lurch forwards.

"Hook!" called the neat man again, louder this time. The monster hesitated then once more lurched forward.

"*Arrêtez!*"

The dead eyes flickered and looked puzzled and he stopped. He looked around uncertainly then shuffled backwards and leant against the door. His right hand came across and pulled mindlessly on the hook on his left, twisting it back and forth. It was not a comforting sight. Both Todd and I were sobering rapidly.

The other man turned his attention unhurriedly back to us. "My name," he said in a precise, educated voice, "is Abraham Mendez. I am come from Mr Jonathan Wild."

Todd and I tore our eyes away from the horror by the door and gave him our full attention. Everyone in London knew Jonathan Wild. He controlled a great deal of the crime in the city and was feared by thieves everywhere.

Abraham noted our reaction and nodded. "I see you know who he is," he said, which was a rhetorical statement if I ever heard one.

"Before I go any further," he continued, " I wish to explain about Hook so that there will be no misunderstandings."

The monster gave no sign of having heard, nor did Abraham acknowledge him in any way.

"Hook is a very sick man. His mind is deranged. He is only in marginal control of himself. I am only marginally in control of him. I could make him become violent but I could not then stop him. Do you understand?"

We understood all too well. My gut was knotted tight and from the greenish look on Todd's face he felt the same way. We both nodded mutely.

"Good. To business. This morning you stole a pocketbook from a young gentleman. As well as money, it has important papers in it. The young gentleman has asked Mr Wild to retrieve them. You were observed and will give the pocketbook to me."

I don't think I even considered disobeying and it wasn't just Hook, although God knows he was enough. Instinctively, I knew that neat men with quiet, confident voices were infinitely more dangerous than monsters. They are either sure of their power, or mad, or both.

Fortunately for our continued good health, we had not discarded the pocketbook. We had considered doing so – the papers were after all of little use to us – but in the end had kept it as convenient holder for the money. Todd took it carefully out of his pocket and handed it across. His hand was trembling badly but Abraham just took the pocketbook without comment and looked inside. All the papers, plus the unspent portion of the money were still there. So, unfortunately, was the banknote which we had not yet converted into cash.

He got to his feet, stowing the pocketbook inside his coat. "You have put me to a great deal of trouble to find you," he said. "I do not want to have to do so again. If you wish to become reader merchants you will inform Mr Wild whenever papers come into your possession and he will see that you are suitably rewarded."

He picked up his hat and the book he had been reading and turned to his companion. "Come, Hook," he said and started towards the door. Hook didn't react. He was looking at us with worrying intensity and his remaining claw-like hand was clenched into a tight, trembling fist. He lurched away from the door towards us.

"*Avec moi, Hook. Venez!*"

Hook hesitated, half turned to follow, then turned back to us. His pupils were dilating rapidly and small bubbles of spittle started to form around his mouth.

"No Sebastian," said Abraham under his breath. Both Todd and I pressed ourselves desperately back against the wall.

"*Sebastian!*" Abraham called, and for the first time I heard a strain in his voice. "*Venez avec moi, enfant. Votre maman attend.*"

I must have shown my shock for Abraham shot me a fast glance. The light in Hook's eyes died and he looked confused. "*Maman?*" he said plaintively.

"*Attente en bas pour moi, Sebastian,*" said Abraham gently. "*Je serai avec tu.*"

The monster shuffled slowly out the door and down the stairs. Everyone in the room let out a deep breath. Abraham looked at me closely.

"You speak French," he said flatly. "What is your name?"

"Bonenfant," I replied. "Pascal Bonenfant."

"Huguenot family?" he asked.

My parents were of Huguenot stock. Their parents had fled France when Catholic persecution of the Protestant religion became too bad. There had been too many massacres and the Huguenots had left by the tens of thousands, despite being forbidden to do so. As well as English they had taught me the language of their homeland. I nodded.

Abraham looked at me consideringly. "Hook's mind is going," he said. "Sometimes he responds to the language of his childhood."

Todd spoke for the first time since Hook had appeared. "What if he hadn't?"

"You would both be dead. Perhaps me as well, although I was closer to the door."

He nodded and made as if leave, then seemed to change his mind. "As it happens," he said, "I have need of a French speaker. I had someone but he thought he could cheat Mr Wild and so he is now unavailable. Put on some clean clothes and come with me."

"But," I said, bewildered, "what about yourself? Your French is as good as mine. Probably better."

He did not even bother to answer. I investigated the small pile of clothes on the bed, looking for something suitable and not too filthy. Even Todd and I had a few reasonable clothes. London is one huge clothes market. Clothes start with the rich, who pass their clothes on to the merely well-to-do, who wear them for a while then forward them on to the middling sort and so eventually to those of us who lived at the bottom. I picked out a dull, respectable coat and some mostly clean stockings – I had no desire to attract the attention of Jonathan Wild.

When I was dressed I accompanied Abraham back down the stairs to where a shivering glimjack was waiting with his torch. In London, the darkness was only held back if the moon was full and there were no clouds.

There was plenty of work for boys brave enough to carry a torch through the filthy and dangerous streets.

This particular boy was backed against the wall, staring at Hook in terror. Hook slowly turned his head towards us and grunted. Abraham indicated to the boy that we should move on and our strange group set off up the dark street – one terrified boy with a shaking torch, one bewildered thief, one enigmatic Jew and one lurching, shambling monster.

Want to read more? *The Unfortunate Deaths of Jonathan Wild* is available now at www.amazon.com in both eBook and print formats.